Interactive Press
Riverside

Ray Liversidge has had his poetry appear in over 100 journals and anthologies in Australia, the US, Canada, the UK, Scotland, Ireland and Spain. His verse novel The Barrier Range was adapted for stage and performed as *Seeking Fabled Waters* at the 2010 Melbourne Writers Festival. In that year his poem 'The Lawn' won the Bruce Dawe National Poetry Prize and was recommended in the Rosemary Dobson Prize. His poems have won and been placed in numerous other competitions. He has been a guest of and read at more than 50 literary festivals in Australia and overseas. See more about Ray at www.poetray.wordpress.com

Interactive Press
Brisbane

Photo: Terri Redpath

Riverside

New & Selected Work
2003-2025

Ray Liversidge

Interactive Press
an imprint of IP (Interactive Publications Pty Ltd)
Treetop Studio • 9 Kuhler Court
Carindale, Queensland, Australia 4152
sales@ipoz.biz
https://ipoz.biz/

© 2025, Ray Liversidge (text) and IP (design)
eBook versions © 2025

All rights reserved. Without limiting the rights under copyright reserved above, no part of this publication may be reproduced, stored in or introduced into a retrieval system, or transmitted, in any form or by any means (electronic, mechanical, photocopying, recording or otherwise), without the prior written permission of the copyright owner and the publisher of this book.

Printed in 12 pt Adobe Caslon Pro on 14 pt Avenir Book.

ISBN: 9781923435148 (PB); 9781923435155 (eBk)

 A catalogue record for this book is available from the National Library of Australia

Acknowledgements

Grateful acknowledgement is made to the editors and publishers of magazines and newspapers in which poems and flash fiction have appeared:
101 Words (USA), the *Adas Anthology*, *Agenda* (UK), *Antipodes* (USA), *Arena*, *ArtStreams*, *Australian Multicultural Book Review*, *Australian Poetry Members Anthology*, *Best Australian Poems*, *Blue Dog*, *Bluepepper*, *Brand* (UK), the *Brisbane Courier Mail*, the *Broadkill Review* (USA), *bystander*, the *Canberra Times*, *Coppertales*, *Cordite*, *Divan*, the *Famous Reporter*, *Fierce Invalids Anthology*, *Five Bells*, *four W eighteen*, *four W ten*, *Gathering Force*, *Going Down Swinging*, *Heartland*, *Husk*, *Inscribe*, *Island*, *Leaf Press*, *LiNQ*, *Lip Service*, *Live Encounters Humour Poetry Anthology*, *Mountain Secrets Anthology*, *Musings During a Time of Pandemic Anthology* (Kenya), *Naugatuck River Review* (USA), *Notata*, *Northern Perspective*, *Off the Path Anthology*, *On Common Water Anthology*, *one-eighth vulture* (SCO), *Oz Poet* website, *Painted Words*, *Parenting Express*, *Permafrost* (USA), *Poetry Australia*, *Poetry Matters*, *Redoubt*, *Reflecting on Melbourne*, *Rocky Hill Lines*, *RumbleFish* (USA), *Said the Rat Anthology*, *Short and Twisted*, *Skylab Visual Poetry* (USA), *Salt-Lick Quarterly*, *Sextuality Anthology*, *SideWaLK*, *Small Packages*, the *Small Times*, *SPUNC*, the *Subterranean*, the *Sydney Morning Herald*, *This Vision Thing Anthology*, *To End All Wars Anthology*, *Ukraine: A World Anthology of Poems on War*, *Ulitarra*, *Verso*, *Westerly*.

Publisher's note: Grateful acknowledgement is made to the editors and publishers of the books in which poems and flash fiction have appeared: *Obeying the Call* (Ginninderra Press 2003), *The Barrier Range* (Flat Chat Press 2006), *Triptych Poets* (Blemish Books 2010), *The Divorce Papers* (Mark Time Books 2010), *no suspicious circumstances* (Littlefox Press 2012), *Oradour-sur-Glane* (Littlefox Press 2017), *…of a sudden* (Ginninderra Press 2023).

Author's Note

Writers are often asked why they write, and poets often asked why poetry. I took on board Seamus Heaney's observation that he doesn't write because he must but because he can, and I consider myself fortunate that I can write and that publishers continue to value and support my work.

As well as being asked why we write, poets are also often asked what poetry is and/or what does it do. Personally, I avoid this navel gazing, but I do like these few quotes:

> *Poetry is a momentary stay against confusion*
> – Robert Frost

> *Art is not an email. It's not supposed to send a message*
> – David Cronenberg

> *A poem should not mean/But be*
> – Archibald MacLeish

Poems and flash fiction in this collection – other than new works - have appeared in my published books and Issue One of *Triptych Poets* (2010). Those published books comprise a collection of poems and flash fiction, three books of poetry, a verse novel and a chapbook.

My first book *Obeying the Call* (2003) covered a range of topics but mostly explored personal and family relationships. While some of the poems are in traditional form such as the sonnet and villanelle, most of the book is written in vers libre.

My next book was the verse novel *The Barrier Range* (2006). Although the book is about a personal journey to find an estranged uncle in Broken Hill, NSW, it is also the imaginative retelling of the 19th century expeditions of explorers Burke and Wills, and Charles Sturt. The book also touches on the dispossession and displacement of Aboriginal peoples from early Australian frontier settlement. Poetry drives the narrative; however other writing genres such as letters, newspaper articles and diary extracts are employed to enhance and enrich the story.

The book uses time shifts to bring knowledge and understanding of current culture to the chronicle of events.

The chapbook *The Divorce Papers* (2010) is a suite of poems concerning my experience of divorce. These poems – as well as several others – appeared in Issue One of *Triptych Poets* (2010).

My third full length collection *no suspicious circumstances: portraits of poets (dead)* (2012) consists of poems about poets who died because of intemperate living, had taken their own lives, or were killed in circumstances out of their control. I chose to adapt the nine-line Spenserian stanza, a fixed verse form invented by Edmund Spenser, where each stanza contains nine lines in total: eight lines in iambic pentameter followed by a single in iambic hexameter. I was drawn to the challenge of this form as I felt it was well suited to my subject matter with its stately and meditative alexandrine final line seemingly an ideal means of saying goodbye to the world.

Oradour-sur-Glane (2017) is about the massacre of 642 people in France in WW2 and the occupation of Paris by the Nazis. I visited the ruined village prior to writing the book, and the poems are not mere depictions of the massacre but rather attempts to capture emotional responses to the senseless suffering, loss and horror of war.

My latest book *...of a sudden* (2023) is a mixture of short poems and flash fiction pieces. This type of fiction is also known micro or sudden, hence the title of my book.

From the above description of my books, I hope it demonstrates my willingness to experiment with something different; challenges I have welcomed with each new project.

I imagine I am no different from any other poet faced with choosing which poems to include in a New & Selected. It is an unenviable task. First collections can often vary in quality, so selecting poems from *Obeying the Call* was relatively easy. Some jumped out at me as I recalled how popular they were with audiences.

The Barrier Range presented more challenges as I wanted to have a selection of the several writing genres I used in the book.

Discovering new poets when conducting research for *no suspicious circumstances: portraits of poets (dead)* was one of the joys of writing this book. Again, some poems chose themselves, remembering the warm reception they received at readings.

When writing *Oradour-sur-Glane* I found the subject matter predicated some passages of reportage. While important to the book's structure, I was conscious of choosing pieces which were more impactful.

With *…of a sudden* I wanted to mainly include pieces which illustrate the wry, irreverent and muted tone of a lot of my work.

Finally, onto the reason for the title of this collection: *Riverside*. Until 2018, I lived all my life in suburban Melbourne. Since that year I have resided in Warrnambool, a city in southwest Victoria. In 2020, my wife and I purchased a house overlooking the Hopkins River. Since then I have written many poems and flash fiction pieces featuring the river. When choosing pieces for this collection I noticed that water appeared in many poems written prior to moving to Warrnambool. So, I thought that *Riverside* was an appropriate title for the collection. The word also has echoes of my surname in it!

I hope that you can enjoy the contents of this collection no matter where you live.

– Ray Liversidge

for my granddaughter, Lola Valentine Liversidge

Contents

NEW	1
T. h. moluccanus	3
On hearing the news that she has won the Pulitzer Prize, Elizabeth Bishop celebrates by consuming not one, but two Oreos	4
So sorry for your loss	5
Everybody wants	6
So, tell me what it is	7
The rent veil	8
Saint Eulalia	9
Machete	11
If I were to	12
The rent veil 2	13
Medi(t)ation	14
He couldn't sleep	16
What time is it?	18
Into the You Beaut Country	20
A folk or fairy tale	22
Half empty/half full	23
The lake	24
Words slowly	26
One day	27
This story may be as tall as the object stolen.	28
The room	29
Measured	31
Like a game	32
The son remembers	33
The Gloaming	34
Reversal of fortune	35
The budding poet	36
Never trust a poet at the wheel	37
Lines referenced in Cento	38
OBEYING THE CALL	41
The company of spiders	43
Blackbirds & nightingales	44
Blackbirds & nightingales 2	47

Animal farm	48
A change in the weather	49
Friday night at the Apollo Milk Bar	50
Love hurts	52
To rhyme with water	53
Ash Wednesday	54
Whales	56
Reef dreaming	57
Deliverance	58
Baudelaire the bricklayer	60
The bowl	62
Postmodern blues	63
Travelling north	65
Chrome	67
Café society	69
The dream	71
Remembering Hiroshima	72
Obeying the call	73

THE BARRIER RANGE — 75

Notes on *The Barrier Range*	76
Draft of Letter to Mr. John Macadam, Honorary Secretary, Exploration Committee, Royal Society of Victoria	77
The aesthetics of disappearance	86
You've got mail	88
Nothing but about the boat	92
Hill of mullock	96
the edge of sundown	100
Mutawintji	111
No news is not good news	118
Menu	123
Check out at the lights, man	124

TRIPTYCH POETS — 129

Things to (and not to) do	131
A corner store, another world	132
The baby and the bathwater	133
The lawn	134
Familial faces	135

A month of Sundays	137
Goya's Dog	138
The Divorce Papers	139

NO SUSPICIOUS CIRCUMSTANCES 147

Singing in chains like the sea	
(Portrait of Dylan Thomas)	149
The path ends where the wood ends	
(Portrait of Edward Thomas)	150
No trembler in the world's storm-troubled sphere	
(Portrait of Emily Brontë)	151
The black sheep of the moor	
(Portrait of Patrick Brontë)	152
All that jazz	
(Portrait of Hart Crane)	153
Days of wine and roses	
(Portrait of Ernest Dowson)	154
A name writ in water	
(Portrait of John Keats)	155
Rilke's wingman	
(Portrait of Sidney Keyes)	156
Piss elegant flâneur	
(Portrait of Shelton Lea)	157
God's parle with dust	
(Portrait of Charlotte Mew)	158
Puttin' on the Ritz	
(Portrait of Edna St Vincent Millay)	159
The art of dying	
(Portrait of Sylvia Plath)	160
Once upon a midnight dreary	
(Portrait of Edgar Allan Poe)	161
Poète maudit	
(Portrait of Arthur Rimbaud)	162
Gravity and waggery	
(Portrait of Christopher Smart)	163
We are all in the gutter, but some of us are looking at the stars	
(Portrait of Oscar Wilde)	164

ORADOUR-SUR-GLANE 165

Oradour-sur-Glane 167

…OF A SUDDEN 173

One wonders 175
Sometimes I don't feel comfortable writing 176
It is hoped this story 177
Imagine if you can this story 178
She had positioned herself 179
Ask you (said quickly) 180
She said: 181
He loved live theatre and bled easily. 182
'What side of the bed do you want?' he asked her. 183
White angels 184
I have put the child 185
Requiem 186
Since 2011 Melbourne, Australia, has 187
For him every month is 188
She lived in the moment and had no sense of history. 189
CO~~RONAVIRUSDISEASE~~ – ~~20~~19 190
He hinted he might consider moving 191

NEW

T. h. moluccanus

On some mornings they could be seen in the trees outside our bedroom glass doors which open onto the back garden.
                              Rather, heard first,
then glimpsed amidst branches of the virgilia. The angle was better from
my side of the bed; but then, over time, it was understood
that you were more than happy with the view
                              from where you were.

Raking the lawn early one spring morning and I catch
the shifting hues of something among
                              the untold purple flowers.
At first, the bird looks like it's roosting, its colourful body
softly rocking. Yet, something is wrong. The red and yellow
feathers of its breast upturned,
                              like the bright blue head is.

I gently prod it with my finger, and the bird topples over.
As it struggles to regain its footing,
                              the lorikeet is already
in my poem, a crumpled rainbow. If I were to turn
around I would see you standing at the bedroom window.
The bird, back on its feet, is looking up into
                              the unbroken blue of the sky.

On hearing the news that she has won the Pulitzer Prize, Elizabeth Bishop celebrates by consuming not one, but two Oreos

Having caught it
you now want to return
this tremendous fish
to the sea. But it's
been filleted and
fried, grilled and
anthologized
to death.
       No matter,
it was an ugly fish
– what with several hooks
through its lower lip –
and its loss is no disaster.

The ocean is vaster
than imagined, so
how easy it can be
to miss the light
flickering on
the dinted bow of your boat.
Your rainbowed boat
of which you are master.

So sorry for your loss

They chase ambulances but never catch
them for death is an abstract concept.
They flock to houses, places of
untold violence, unthinkable infant deaths,
but never arrive in time to stop it. So,
they leave flowers and candles and teddy bears
and homemade cards with heartfelt condolences
written on them.
                    Grief thieves, they circle like vultures
round hearses, churches, graves and funeral parlours.
Empty and surrendered vessels longing to be
the loudest, the most redeemed.

Thank you for coming.

Everybody wants

their Johnny Cash moment. Everybody wants to see the light.

In 1967 Johnny Cash entered the Nickajack Cave in Marion County, Tennessee, intent on not coming out.

He may or may not have known that in the late 1700s the river and the cave were controlled by the Chickamauga Cherokees until a number of them were killed in a surprise attack by American frontiersmen on 13 September 1794. Shortly after, the Chickamaugas signed a peace treaty.

The batteries in Johnny Cash's flashlight gave out and the man in black was in the cave in the dark for some three hours before he glimpsed the light at the entrance to the cave and saw the light of God. He found a line out of the cave and walked it.

Historically, the cave has housed a colony of grey bats. Today, the cave is a wildlife refuge.

If I were to have a Johnny Cash moment – and had a choice – I would take the light, literally.

So, tell me what it is

you heard, and what you know
of the world?
Have you fallen asleep
inside your life – again?
Does the future look like silence?
The present taste of fear?
Is the past feculent with regret?
Do you revisit the past
or does it revisit you?
I'll tell you what the narrative is.
I'll tell you how the narrative goes.
Landscapes collide. Plates shift.
Rivers dry up.
You seek fabled waters
you once glimpsed only to
have them disappear, or
maybe they were never there,
or always liminal.

The rent veil

LIVEVILEVILIVEVILIVEVILEVILIVE
LIVEVILEVILIVEVILIVEVILEVILIVE
LIVEVILEVILIVEVILIVEVILEVILIVE
LIVEVILEVIL   VILEVILIVE
LIVEVILEVIL LIVE VILEVILIVE
LIVEVILEVIL I V   VILEVILIVE
LIVEVILEVIL V I   VILEVILIVE
LIVEVILEVIL EVIL VILEVILIVE
LIVEVILEVIL   VILEVILIVE
LIVEVILEVILIVEVILIVEVILEVILIVE
LIVEVILEVILIVEVILIVEVILEVILIVE
LIVEVILEVILIVEVILIVEVILEVILI   VEIL

Saint Eulalia

None of my sufferings has been equal to that of not having suffered enough.
– Saint Margaret Mary Alacoque

And now, ladies and gentlemen,
For your entertainment, please
Give it up for our youngest
Contestant all the way from
Barcelona, the born to be canonized,
The one, the only EU-LA-LI-A!

Bring it on!
Bring on your implements,
Your contemptible playthings,
Maximian, Roman scum!
For nothing offends me more
Than your many gods,
Your animal sacrifices,
Your offer of frankincense,
Your reality TV.
Here, cop a gob of phlegm.
Bring on your sport.
My body holds no mystery.

Trophies of Christ
The number of hooks
Inserted under my skin,
My exposed bone already
A relic; my ascending breasts
Suckled in heaven,
My burnt flesh
A seductive perfume,
My severed head nestled
On the chest of Jesus,
My crucified and

Butchered body a temple
Of bloody sacraments.

Spoiler Alert.
For her final act
Our celebrity guest
Will have a dove fly
From her mouth, snow
Fall on her naked body.

Machete

(Muh-shet-ee)

Muh
a muffled grunt
as the arm commences
its arc

shet
the convergence of metal
and flesh

ee
his final breath

If I were to

find myself in a shootout and if I were to hold the gun horizontally rather than vertically I would like to believe ballistically the trajectory of the bullet would increase exponentially to the passiveness of my language and kill the motherfucker before he would have me killed.

The rent veil 2

```
              LIVEVILIVE
              LIVEVILIVE
              LIVEVILIVE
              LIVEVILIVE
LIVEVILEVILIVEVILIVEVILEVILIVE
LIVEVILEVIL   LIVE    VILEVILIVE
LIVEVILEVIL   I  V    VILEVILIVE
LIVEVILEVIL   V  I    VILEVILIVE
LIVEVILEVIL   EVIL    VILEVILIVE
LIVEVILEVILIVEVILIVEVILEVILIVE
              LIVEVILIVE
              LIVEVILIVE
              LIVEVILIVE
              LIVEVILIVE
              LIVEVILIVE
              LIVEVILIVE
              LIVEVILIVE
              LIVEVILIVE
              LIVEVILIVE
              LIVEVILI   VEIL
```

Medi(t)ation

A comfortable seated position
is recommended, with a suggestion
to breathe (the good) in
through the nose and
(the bad) out through the mouth.
So, I take deep breaths,
resisting, each time, to hold
for too long.

Encouragement is given
to sending comity to others
(including yourself).

May we all be happy.
As in:
birthday | anniversary | easter |
new year | hanukkah | ramadan |
holidays | Hammond | Gilmore |
as Larry | slapper | clapper |
hashtag | as can be | for you |
to be here | to be of help | as a pig in |
(Add more here).

May we all be healthy.
As in:
appetite | attitude | hashtag |
diet | deity | lifestyle |
food |
(Add more here).

May we all be free from suffering.
As in:
sexual abuse | domestic violence | detention |
ethnic cleansing | police brutality | racism |
sexism | homophobia | an overdose |
a relapse | fools gladly | the little children to come unto |
from suffering |
(Please add more here).

Prompted to wriggle fingers and
toes to leave the other world,
you return to the room you are sitting in.
The Zoom session comes to an end
at the tolling of the bell.

He couldn't sleep

so he left his wife in bed and quietly made his way to the lounge room. It was the witching hour but his mind – conditioned by many years of disappointment – was at a level of scepticism whereby he did not expect to be visited by a paranormal. And the times of babies waking at such an ungodly hour were but a vague memory.

He sat in his armchair, turned on the reading light, and picked up a copy of *New Scientist*. He perused an article on autism which made him question his state of being given his repetitive behaviours and restricted interests. He was relieved to read further in the article that adults cannot suddenly develop the disorder.

He put down the magazine and turned off the lamp. As his chair faced the television, the first thing he saw when he opened his eyes was the red standby light. He wasn't sure how long he had been asleep, but he assumed it was only for a short time as it was still dark. He thought of picking up the remote but instead continued to look at the light on the TV. How many times had he found himself in this position? Not just the corporeality of sitting in his chair staring at a blank or populated screen, but again being at a point where his life had flat lined.

When his first marriage failed, he swore never to again build or buy a house on two levels. In the early years, it was somewhat of a novelty to know his wife was in the kitchen upstairs while he watched TV in the room below. After the divorce, he liked to joke to his friends that his wife left him because they were literally and figuratively on different levels.

When his second wife told him that she wanted out of their relationship, she did so from the kitchen which was on the same level as the lounge room from where he watched television. He pressed the mute button on the remote and walked over to the island bench where his wife was dicing vegetables.

'Tell me one thing you've contributed to this marriage?'

He hadn't anticipated such a question, just as he didn't see the end of this marriage – and, for that matter, his first marriage – coming. From experience, he knew the seven stages of grief, and that at this very moment he was in a state of disbelief. His mind – like the screen of a TV which has been turned off – went blank. Then it flickered, but he understood that from where he was the reception was poor. A test pattern briefly appeared, only to be replaced by white noise. He knew he needed to take control. Take the control and fast forward this moment, rewind and pause other times in his life. Delete scenes in which he had acted badly.

Later, he would write a list of things he might have said in answer to his wife's question, but for now all he could think of was when, on the occasion of their last anniversary, he had surprised her with a 165cm television.

What time is it?

He turns to look at the digital clock. 2:22.

Have you been awake long?

Not long.

Is it me?

No.

Is there something on your mind?

No.

What are you reading?

Our Strangers.

Who's it by?

Lydia Davis.

Don't know her. Is it good?

Yeah, it's good.

Just good?

Well, very good.

Please try not to stay up too long.

I won't.

Goodnight.

Goodnight.

When there's a change in her breathing, he puts down the book and reaches for his phone.

Into the You Beaut Country

for John Olsen

One can make a day of any size, and regulate the rising and setting of his own sun and the brightness of its shining
- John Muir

walking for sixty years
                or more
                            Paul Klee's line
quizzical squiggles
              anguine wriggle
     crossing cancroid night by river
crinkum-
      crankum
            channel country

gone grounds foremiddleback
                        in lieu
        eye of bird
      foot of frog
riparian brown
        god almighty blue
     spots of time
                    tide

              there
                  Theodore Roethke's 'squirmers
        in bogs and bacterial creepers'
here
   Seamus Heaney's 'slobber of frogspawn'
      growing like 'clotted water
              in the shade of the banks'
cadmium-yellow of sun (egg)
          cerulean blues

```
billabong    spoonbill    lillypond    pond
       dragonfly    lagoon    polliwog    tadpole
                      frog
                         frog
                            frog
                               froggery of frogs
tributary
      then tributary
          now estuarine
                     ripple
                    popple
       spilth of memory
                    Bondi beach
          a bucket      a boy        blue bottles popping
```

A folk or fairy tale

The homosexuals in Australia, they took the word gay.
– Bob Katter

Once was enough to be upon
a time in a land as unlit as this.
Here, the tropes were as bloated as
any from a folk or fairy tale:
all Queens deemed evil,
all dragons an affront to civility.

After a period of unrest,
the King called for calm.
No questions would be asked
and no punishment given
if the rainbow was returned
and the appropriated word
repositioned to its rightful place
in the lexicon hierarchy
so that all the people
and not just a minority
could once again feel free to be
as the word which rhymes
with my given name.

Half empty/half full

Blink and you will miss it:
Mist sheeting in from sea,
Over hill, ghosting the river.

As soon as he steps onto the
Balcony the seagulls swoop,
Expecting scraps. He does
Not really care for the birds
Yet evening finds him
In a pantomime not knowing
When it began or will end.
She comes with two glasses
Of wine and he thinks they look
Half empty. She knows they are half full.

Blink again and you will miss it
Just as quickly lifting.

The lake

She takes the path down to the lake, past the abandoned cars in the field.
Last year, the sudden arrival of the first car had surprised her.
                                        Now it was rusting and,
as happens, newly dumped sedans and hatchbacks dot the landscape
                                  like way-too focussed haystacks.
Already the sun's fiery utterance has silenced the natural world.
A sticker peeling from a rear window reminds her of the post-it
she left for him.
                                      No matter what happens
he will want his muesli,
           and as she runs her hand over a tyre with no tread

she wonders if he will get it right and see the note among
the many fridge magnet
homilies and Leunig cartoons littering the refrigerator door.
                                Earlier, it seemed the paper boy
had issued in a new age with a flourish of his arm –
                      but it proved a false dawn.
Daylight saving had discombobulated the birds, and the rain,
even the early morning rain, had panicked and totally lost it
and gone ballistic
                            on the corrugated iron roof.
When it was over she walked
   by the kangaroo grass and the car wrecks and down to the lake.

He finished his muesli in silence, resisting the temptation to listen
to talkback radio.
The distinctive croak of a Pobblebonk frog sounded in the distance,
                                        and he reasoned
she had waited for the rain to stop before leaving the house.
                            At the end of the day,

she had said to him the previous night, at the end of the day
we are each of us alone.
At the end of the day, he replied, the sun sets.
                And with that, she walked into the bedroom,
closing the door behind her.
                        Poetry speaks against our vanishing.

She is thinking how it is a common trope in Shakespeare's sonnets
when she spots him moving
among the discarded bodies of the cars.
                Something in the trees makes the sound
of a minor piano key as she waits for the fall of his footsteps
                        on the underwood to dispel
her silent chanting of the stations. Two cormorants settle on the lake
disassembling the upside
down holiday house.
          He thinks of Tony Soprano and the paddling of ducks
in his pool. And, like the mobster,
is disarmed by dread
                wondering how they know when it's time to go.

Words slowly

Words slowly, ever so slowly, return.
Orphaned, over time, by love, made homeless
By fire, they sheltered themselves between
Our fuliginous covers on your library shelves
Patiently waiting to be rediscovered:
Adamson, Akhmatova, Albiston, Auden...
The letters and names and titles reappearing
Like branches of trees through dense fog
Once the soot is swept from our spines.

You could have chosen any one of us
But you sit down with Basho
As you have some losses in common
And it is a long and sinuous road to Zukofsky.
You talk for a while and Basho says how he admires
The line in your poem about a Pobblebonk frog,
Then takes the narrow path down to the pond.

One day

at primary school I practised kissing on a metal pole. A girl I admired, and who I may have been thinking about, was playing hopscotch nearby. I saw her giggle, stop playing the game, and run over to her group of friends.

The metal pole was cold on my lips and tasted bitter and was the same colour as the girl's eyes.

This story may be as tall as the object stolen.

He was a Year 10 art student and in love with his new teacher, Angela Elmsbury. Angela. Elmsbury. Like Lolita, the name rolled around and off his tongue like honey. He longed for life drawing classes but was instead given an assignment on abstract art.

He did his research. He walked around the campus after dark and noticed that not all the windows of the classrooms were closed. Towards the end of the final term he returned one night to the school grounds and climbed through the open window and into the art classroom. He was not an overly strong boy but he managed to carry the easel back to the house where he lived with his parents.

He put the easel in the garage as it was too big for his bedroom. As he looked at it leaning against timber planks and building material he thought of the scene in *Blowup* where the world-weary lead character, initially excited to be gifted with the neck of Jeff Beck's smashed-up guitar, casually discards it on the pavement.

He gave up school after Year 11 and did an apprenticeship in carpentry.

The room

she leaves the room
exactly as it was
the gap between
the mattress and
the wall
the overturned light

she leaves the room
exactly as it
was   the gap
between the mattress
and the wall
the Barbie Doll
fallen to the floor
the overturned
light

she leaves
the room
exactly
as it was
the gap
between the
mattress and
the wall
the Barbie Doll
fallen
to the floor
the twisted plastic limbs
the over-
turned
light

she leaves
the room
exactly
as it
was
the gap
between
mattress and wall
her Barbie Doll
falling
her twisted limbs
the turned over
light

she leaves the room
exactly as it is
the gap between
the light overturned

she leaves the room
as it is

she leaves
the room
as it is

she leaves
the room

she leaves

the room

Measured

We are measured in so many ways:
Against doorjambs or walls when young,
By fads and fashion in our teens,
By others as we age.

Who can say at what point pencil marks
Were painted over, when bald and shaven
Heads became chic, 80 the new 60,
And whether it really matters.

My father would laugh like a torn
Chaff bag, talk and talk some more
So not, I fear, to know what silence holds.

When my mother died my father
Migrated like a bird to the place
Where a felled tree stood.

Our looted shrines and
Emptied temples belittle us,
And I am measured in response.

Like a game

of lotto, a marble dropped with his name on it. And, like Muhammad Ali, he had no quarrel with them Viet Cong. He was a lover, not a fighter, and he was prepared to do time for his beliefs rather than military service. Fearful youths whose number had come up were self-harming in the hope of failing the medical exam. Only days before his appointment he got an abscess in his ear which caused so much pain it passed all his understanding. When he met with the medical staff he was accused of using a rusty nail to cause infection. It was a common ploy, they said, along with shooting off a toe.

He sat in the waiting room with nine other conscripts. The conversation circled like a helicopter for some time before landing on the question of those willing to go and those not. If the voting in the room that day was a litmus test of that city, that state, that country, then it showed that 80% of conscripts were prepared to undertake national service.

Some conscientious objectors were gaoled during the time of the National Service Scheme, including Simon Townsend, producer and host of the television program Simon Townsend's Wonder World! Townsend was accompanied on the show by his pet and companion bloodhound, Woodrow. This gave the he of our story an idea. He will never know if his abscessed ear or his confessed unconditional love for his dog convinced the medical team that he did 'not meet the standards of fitness required of persons called upon to render service under the National Service Act.'

Many times during the forty-seven years since he received the letter from the Department of Labour and National Service, he had felt a kind of sense of duty to put it in a frame and prominently display it in the house somewhere. Over that time, however, many more wars have come and gone, and with each one his interest in displaying the letter diminished.

The son remembers

them as ordinary parents who went quietly about their lives. Comfortably numb, as Pink Floyd lyricized.

His mother tolerated her husband's habit of riding his hobby horse: the misery all levels of government inflict on the community. He tolerated her smoking.

She died first. The senior citizens theatrical group were rehearsing for an upcoming show when she faltered on a simple dance step and dropped dead on stage.

At some point, elderly couples have the discussion of what to do when one of them dies first. She knew her smoking had affected her lung and heart, but she kept it a secret. So, she figured she would most likely be the one to go first and told her husband if that were to eventuate, then she had chosen a widow from the theatrical group to look after him.

The couple spent time in each other's company but never lived together. After about six months, she tired of him regularly mounting his hobby horse, and one warm summer evening she fed the horse a carrot and then walked off into the sunset.

Soon after, the hobby horse – bereft of an audience – panicked and bucked, throwing the rider to his death.

The son never did find out what his father suggested his mother do in his absence.

The Gloaming

the Celtic breath
              intimates
                          death
  suggests
      a brokered heart
    sold down
  the Liffey

language is
              its own tongue

flames reel
        from the fiddle
the fiddler nods
            to the holder
    of the hardanger
               to quell the fire

fire quelled
        the guitarist
               fingers the flames

from the other
            side of the stage
        another part
    of the world
                        a counterpointing
                      piano

unnoticed
        the singer
              has ceased
                    singing

Reversal of fortune

He sat on the balcony in darkness, a forefinger
tracing the rim of the drained glass in his lap,
a spent bottle by his side.

Earlier, he took the half-empty bottle of whiskey
from the cabinet and poured himself a drink.

Earlier, he was about to call his mother with the news
before remembering she had died two months ago.

Earlier, the grandfather clock in the hall chimed
nine times which was the reminder for him to read a story
to his son and his daughter before they went to sleep.

Earlier, the thought of eating briefly crossed his mind
when he stared vacantly into the space where the
dining room table and four chairs once stood.

Earlier, he received a text message at the
very moment he entered the house to find
most of the furniture and his family gone.

Earlier, after leaving work, he expected his wife
to hand him a glass of wine when he walked in the door.

Earlier, her customary morning goodbye kiss had seemed
somewhat perfunctory, but he paid it no mind.

Earlier, the day had begun like any other.

The budding poet

was beside himself with joy when for the first time he had a poem accepted for a small magazine. To his surprise he had another poem accepted for the next issue. The more the monthly magazine continued to publish his poems the more he came to believe that – although the magazine didn't pay and all other magazines had rejected his work – he might one day be able to give up his day job and write full time.

Over time he got to know the editor. One night over a few drinks the poet asked the editor how he got into the publishing business. The editor told the poet that after several years of having every poem of his rejected, he realised that the only way he would get published was to start his own magazine.

After a fourth pint the editor confessed to the poet that the first issue of the magazine compromised poems under his name and several pseudonyms. He then started receiving submissions from other poets which he published in future issues.

The editor ordered two whiskeys to celebrate the success of the magazine. No poet should have to go through what I did he said. That's why I don't reject any poems sent to me he told the poet.

Never trust a poet at the wheel

(A cento)

They bring their wounded sonnets
And their collapsed blank verses.
Some start playing tennis with the net down,
Others wait for a ball to be thrown in from nowhere.
Sometimes you donkey-plod along…
Then suddenly the gods are onside.
Then, O how the waters come down at Lahore.
Yet, anxiety can drive you to an excess of commas.
Try staring at the lighted window and just breathe.
So long as there are new purposes for rope
There will always be new knots to discover.
The lyf so short, the craft so long to lerne.
Yet, life and the things that happen to us know no celebrity,
Or maybe it's just a bunch of stuff that happens.
If you find it insisting upon itself,
Marvel at the cruel complacency of ordinary things
And try to give the mundane its beautiful due.
Art is not an email. It's not supposed to send a message.
And remember, never trust a poet at the wheel.
If he can drive, distrust the poems.

Lines referenced in Cento

They bring their wounded sonnets
And their collapsed blank verses.
'They bring their wounded sonnets and their spastic sestinas and their collapsed blank verses.' – Peter Porter from an interview in The Age (17/7/99) discussing writing classes and workshops.

Some start playing tennis with the net down,
'Free verse is like playing tennis with the net down.' – Robert Frost.

Others wait for a ball to be thrown in from nowhere.
'Now and then a poem comes like that, like a ball kicked in from nowhere.' – Seamus Heaney.

Sometimes you donkey-plod along...
Then suddenly the gods are onside.
'Sometimes you can donkey-plod around...then suddenly the gods are onside.' – Brett Whiteley.

Then, O how the waters come down at Lahore.
'O how the waters come down at Lahore.' – from Ulysses by James Joyce.

Yet, anxiety can drive you to an excess of commas.
'Anxiety drives me to an excess of commas.' – Patrick White.

Try staring at the lighted window and just breathe.
'Stare at the lighted window and just breathe.' – from Staring at the Sun by Julian Barnes.

So long as there are new purposes for rope
There will always be new knots to discover.
from The Ashley Book of Knots by Clifford Warren Ashley.

The lyf so short, the craft so long to lerne.
– Geoffrey Chaucer.

Yet, life and the things that happen to us know no celebrity,
'Life and the things that happen to us know no celebrity.' – Patti Smith.

Or maybe it's just a bunch of stuff that happens.
'It's just a bunch of stuff that happened.' – Homer Simpson in The Simpsons dismissing suggestions a story he tells has a moral.

If you find it insisting upon itself,
'It insists upon itself.' – Peter Griffin in The Family Guy discussing The Godfather film.

Marvel at the cruel complacency of ordinary things
'Marvelling at the cruel complacency of ordinary things.' – from The Sea *by John Banville.*

And try to give the mundane its beautiful due.
'To give the mundane its beautiful due.' – John Updike, explaining his reason for writing.

Art is not an email. It's not supposed to send a message.
– David Cronenberg.

And remember, never trust a poet at the wheel.
If he can drive, distrust the poems.
'Never trust a poet at the wheel. If he can drive, distrust the poems.' – from The Information *by Martin Amis.*

OBEYING THE CALL

2003

The company of spiders

The spider finds a home
on the kitchen windowsill

suspended among glass
bottles and jars.

A mandala pregnant with meaning
she squats and waits –

her back bubbling with unborn babies.
By morning her children are leaving

the dead body and moving out
from the centre of the web

along delicate threads
to the circle's rim.

'You can't just leave them there!'
my daughter protests,

arms flailing, hands flapping,
while her brother suggests

flushing them down the sink.
As the children ready for school,

I take the jar outside,
place it in the garden

amongst fallen bark and snowgrass,
and linger in the company of spiders.

Blackbirds & nightingales

1.

the pressure
finally

too much
to bear

together we
seek relief

return
without a word

to the cold
comfort of bed

resuming
spoony postures

in the dark
I lie awake

listening to
the slow

diminuendo
of chthonic water

is that your stomach
or is it mine?

the earth turns
on its side

and answers
with a sigh

blinded to
the view I have

not of stars
bedimmed by apathy

but a galaxy
obscenely meretricious

a moon lewd
with light

culpably silent

2.

wasted by wine
and talk

we sought
solace in bed

forgetting beauty
in pursuit of truth

I found only truth
without charity

mea culpa

3.

and now
as light

falls in
the space

between their
moony shapes

she wakes and
begins to weep

as he cries himself
to sleep

to dream
of nightingales

when blackbirds
are warbling

in the morning heat

Blackbirds & nightingales 2

1.

You sought the strong and silent type,
I played the victim to your stalking beauty.

And when I thought we'd found
The words to say to one another

Your kisses took my breath away,
Your mouth unmanned me in the dark.

For years we slept supinely in our bed,
And blamed each other when we didn't wake.

2.

Born from the knocking dark,
The silent, bloody theatre of expression,

This morning brings birds in quick propinquity
To roost upon a sapling's votive branch,

Their presence more vivid than
Any dream, bright as this love

Which asks only that we kiss,
And call each other by our names.

Animal farm

The farm of old McDonald
Is in our bed this morning.
All manner of bird and beast
Running riot. Last night all was quiet,
Quiet as a mouse: with a squeak
Squeak here, small talk there,
And awkward silence everywhere.
I watch a chicken de-clucked by
A fox's presence, find a real frog
Drowning in an imaginary pond.
Now the sun rises on our nakedness –
The cock that doesn't crow a silent
Reminder from a recent dunghill,
Then the shrill entropy of birdsong.

A change in the weather

I tell her the problem appears to be
In that area there where a trough of low pressure extends
From the Great Dividing Range to the low centred near Tasmania.
Placing her hand on mine
She says she can feel high pressure systems
Moving in from the Bight and the Tasman Sea.
Dripping with perspiration I ask her
If she thinks conditions are likely to remain humid.
Slowly removing her designer T-shirt and skirt
To reveal the latest in two-piece swimwear
She answers that circumstances will remain unchanged
While pressures continue to be exerted in certain places.
Falling back onto my towel I question her about the future.
She says the forecast is for more unstable weather
With the possibility of a late thunderstorm.
And then without warning she leans across and tracing
The outline of my bathers with her finger
Whispers in my ear something about isobars and suggests
That if I don't like the weather at the moment to wait
And it will almost certainly change.

Friday night at the Apollo Milk Bar

It seems the boys are blessed
with serendipity tonight
and celebrate their joy
by sucking on a can of Coke,
lighting up another cigarette,
striking macho poses to shame
even the most curious animal.
For, out of school uniform,
she is Aphrodite in denim,
Madonna in underwear…
any fantasy they want her to be
on this warm November evening.

After placing her reply, she sits
to wait at the green Laminex table.
Through the last O of APOLLO
she notices the older boy in the group
is watching her from the street
while the others cough, guffaw,
and plot in crude and broken English
to do the things that boys are wont to do
at the Apollo Milk Bar after dark.

From the doorway a hand brushes aside
plastic strips; a foot pirouettes
on the linoleum (she feels they see
the sudden shaping in the leg);
then she twists, turns her back on the boys
and walks towards the corner and the waiting car:
the taste of vanilla milkshake in her mouth,
the fried fat of chips on her smiling lips.

As the car disappears into the night
she lets her body slide down the back seat,
satisfied that she has left them,
wondering if it was a wave of the hand
they saw through the rear window
or the head of a toy dog nodding.

Love hurts

Some say I took it from my bag,
And holding it up for him to see
Said something about love,
Then ran the blade along my cheek
Before he had a chance to act.

Others thought they saw me lift
The knife, say something about love,
Then try to slash his handsome face.
He grabbed my hand and bent it back –
And that was when my cheek was cut.

Then there are those who swear
They saw him reach inside his jacket,
And heard him threaten to disfigure me
If love was mentioned once again.
Then his hand was seen to move
Toward my face with something in it.

I admit I can't remember everything
About the party. They say I seemed
A bit on edge that night; and I guess
I smoked and drank a bit too much
To try and calm my nerves.
Yet everyone agreed they'd never seen
Me dance so much and have such fun.

If I no longer laugh it's because
I miss his touch upon my cheek…
And live with the thought of forever bearing
This long and lovely reminder of his smile.

To rhyme with water

If I suggest the beach
is within reach
she says the sea sux.
The local pool?
Uncool.
And when, in anger, I mention
a river near Phoenix…
Well, it's then she begins to cry.
So I drive to a lake in Ballarat
where she quickly runs to a tree
and hides her face in the shade.
After a long silence she walks
down to the water's edge
where I motion her to come in
as I need her
to rhyme with water.
Tossed pebbles summon
rock wood water
then the sound of laughter circling the lake
before breaking at her feet.
'In your face, Dad!'

As day drifts into evening
she comes and sits beside me
on the bank, her hair wet
and dark against the pale skin.
We look at each other,
the pile of pebbles in her palm:
vocables: cool, wicked.

Ash Wednesday

…I made the nights
resound in silence with remembered loving
yet lost you in the grinding daily chores.
– Bruce Beaver

              1.

Summer comes around
soon enough – the next
    bend in fact: the familiar

    shoulder of the hill
dipping into surf,
    the flank bright with the sun

    of the very first day,
and the family cabin
    (like a postcard)

    tucked into the gap
between
    forest and sea.

              2.

The car turns onto the Great Ocean Road.
He's decided he should drive,
so she sits on the side of the forest.

The holiday has ended as it began –
with whimpering children and the flywire
door banging against the jamb.

In Anglesea she notices a house
which wasn't there last year... and sees
young lovers running into the water

hand in hand or walking in the woods
at dusk, the trunks of trees flushed
with light, the leaves thick and shaking

with the *frisson* of stolen moments. Now
days distend with daily chores, while nights
rebound in silence with remembered loving.

'I said it has to be inside the car'.

The lights change at Moorabool Street
as her mind goes back to the forest.

'I spy with my little eye something beginning with f'.
As he did on the trip up, the father
points out the flame at the oil refinery.

On the outskirts of Melbourne, she sees the bare
branches, follows the line of the eucalypt
and finds the fern, its frond unfurling in blackness.

Whales

By now
I'm usually halfway
along the road
– the shouting over,
the crying done –
and about to turn
back to the house
to say sorry again
when the familiar notes
of Carole King's piano
float from your bedroom window
and drift across the bay
like yachts before the wind…
*But it's too late, now darling,
it's too late…*

This time
I continue to
the end of the road
until I reach the bluff.
Below, whales,
like spent emotions, beached
and breathless on the sand.

Reef dreaming

for Sarah

Leaving the boat
you enter the world of water
naked of knowledge –
schooled only in the use
of snorkel, mask and flipper.
At first, uncertain of the ocean's depth,
your arms and legs go everywhere,
the sudden terror in your heart
heard in each troubled breath.
A fish swims in front of you. Then another.
And another. The colours brighter than
the brightest colours in your favourite box of paints.
Now your mouth becomes a gill, limbs
a tail and fins. You drift among reef and fish:
a friend, a fellow fish… until the reef appears
like the living thing it is
to crawl out from the shadows and
seek the light it feeds upon.
Now, caught between coral and the source of light,
fish dreaming turns to fear – you feel the reef
slice into your flesh like a knife, gills
filling with water…

Taking your hand
we find a sand bank
to stand upon, and I explain
how the glass in the mask magnifies the view.
'It changes the look of things', I say.
'Like the mind does when it dreams'.
Still holding hands, we turn
our backs on the reef
and push off for the shore,
floating like lovers on a canvas by Chagall.

Deliverance

When I feel the need
to push

I pant.
Staccato breaths

arrest (temporarily)
the head

butting the dark,
ease the incumbent

flesh, allay the little
agonies of labour

until the quick,
complete surrender

to the weight of
rushing water. And

like water
like fire

the baby comes –
brutal, cruel,

and simply beautiful.
Then the flames

about the flesh
expire, and the body

bruised and bloodied
lies wasted on the bed,

broken like the husk
of some exotic fruit.

And after being blind
at birth

my mind now wakes
and leaps around the room

yet cannot rest or settle
until it holds the child

like vacuum a void
or fire a fever –

a void
only joy can fill,

a fever
only love assuages.

Baudelaire the bricklayer

(After Seamus Heaney's 'Follower')

My father worked like a packhorse.
Striding the grounds he'd survey the site,
Study detailed plans of the house
To be built, his eye a theodolite.

A bloody perfectionist, he'd cock
His head, calculate the gauge, determine
The bond, and drop a plumb line from the top
Of the frame for square, all the while

Looking like a loony with a knotted
Handkerchief for a hat. But he was no fool.
Once a fresh batch of mortar was knocked
Up, he would reach for his tools.

Now his hands moved through air in time
To conduct the scoop and spread of mud,
The lifting and laying and tapping into line
With a hammer, handle or blade

Of the trowel each and every brick
In the walls he called his 'works of art'. Yet I
Failed to see beauty in stacks of bricks
Or a world in a grain of sand, cement or lime.

The building site was a foreign place
Where men spoke another tongue,
Dressed in ridiculous bib-and-brace
Overalls, and whistled songs out of tune.

I never could wear hobnailed boots,
Or take to digging holes with a spade.
'Maybe you'd be better off in a suit,'
He'd say. 'Or learning another trade.'

So I got through the days by reading Baudelaire
And Rimbaud, drinking absinth, deranging the senses,
Deciding that life is elsewhere
While raking joints and mending fences.

I failed to follow in his footsteps,
Slipped sometimes in my sandshoes
From dodging discarded clinkers, broken batts,
Bricks with double frogs, other nomenclatures.

My father was annoying to work with,
Yapping always, always the verb.
Today his walls still cast a shadow in which
I see a boy awkwardly scrawling his first words.

The bowl

Domestic, the memories of mothers.
Forget the faded photo of a girl
On horseback, the wedding shots –
I wasn't there, and I have moved
Beyond the want of rivalry.
While Dad was always 'in his shed'
Or 'out the back somewhere',
You could be found in the kitchen.
We knew what day it was by what we ate.
Yet now I understand why on some days
You refused to cook, cried, threw cutlery,
And called us a 'pack of bastards'
If we answered or didn't answer back.
Your hysteria took root in the word.

When I visit now it's to find you
On a cold and sunless afternoon
Stooped over the stove ladling soup,
The warmth from the hotplate
Holding you for a moment
Before you turn to show your face…
I take the bowl you offer,
The plate of buttered bread.

Postmodern blues

Life is first boredom, then fear
– Philip Larkin

Perhaps you'd like to try that opening line
Again because it's obvious from the way
You dress you don't come here often or get
Out much anymore. And who can blame you?
Statistics show that even as I speak
Somebody's being stabbed or shot or kicked
To death outside a nightclub not unlike
The one you're in. Still you need to get
Out every now and again don't you? I mean
It does you good. You can't stay home all of
The time now can you even if you do run
The risk of getting in a fight and being hit
And suffering serious injury. Yet there's
More chance of being run down by a car
Or struck by lightning don't you think?
Hey you don't say much do you?

                      Oh, but I do.
Or, at least, I once did. Now, what's the point?
Maybe I was married for too long and have lost
The art of conversation. Maybe the method for pulling chicks
Is different now. My ex now marks the spot and I
Find myself in unfamiliar territory, remembering
A street, a house, and lighted windows at dusk.

By now the dinner party guests
Have fallen to impressions of American sitcoms
(Homer himself hath been observ'd to nod… Doh!)
While the boys at the club are thinking of
Getting down to some serious drinking, being full
Of piss and wind, signifying fuck all.

Oh, our podded lives lead only to the softly spoken
Platitudes of hope… Is that the time?
It seems you no sooner settle into a rhythm
You feel comfortable with when the little separations
Begin. Perhaps I'll try that opening line again sometime –
It might just work the second time around.

Travelling north

Some things in life can take an age to shift, or move
So indiscernibly we never see them disappear from view
Or settle gently into place: continental drift;
A tower leaning by degrees; the migratory flight
Of arthritic refugees who leave to seek an endless summer
Here and eternal skies of blue. Instead, they find
Infernal annual heat and ceaseless swarms of flies
In Heaven's waiting room. Still, they seem content to sit
Or stand around at stations or designated locations
And wait for air-conditioned coaches to carry them off
To Dreamworld or into the hinterlands.
                              At twilight time
The world becomes unreal or remains too much with them.
So, they leave their flats to find comfort in the arms
Of strangers on the dance floors of the RSLs,
(Lest we forget), or draw the blinds and stay inside
With a brandy and TV. Yet, before the last
Strains of 'The Last Waltz' end on a discordant note,
And the final glass is lifted to indifferent lips,
They shall have wearied with age – and in the morning
There will be nobody to remember them. Then they find
Themselves remembering them – the dearly departed, that is –
And, when they do, they understand they have survived
To bear the guilt, regret and grief which memory brings.
For the aching joys of youth have gone, and aching joints
And dizzy spells seem insufficient recompense for all
Those years of married life.

                    Now, life is nothing more
Than spent emotions recollected in tranquillity,
Induced by Valium and other pills prescribed
By those who say they have their best interests at heart.

Yet, you tell me who really cares about these sad,
Imbecilic, biddable old biddies who spend their final days
And dollars bent over bowling balls or bingo
Tables waiting for their number to come up?
And they do not come up to Paradise for the fruit,
Or because they're fools, or beasts, or blessed – or for a change.
(For they know the more things change, the more they stay the same).
No, they end up here because they have been condemned
For living longer than some, or living longer than others
Would like them to.
                    We only want to live and die
With dignity. I must go now – I think I've outstayed my welcome.

Chrome

It's good to know we still
can look in others' eyes

without desire or envy,
without the risk of losing

your life, the fear
of recognition. Yet,

most of the time we keep
to ourselves: reading,

sleeping, listening to music,
looking out the window

at houses not our own, thinking
of the ones we love –

or nothing at all. So,
when the train pulls in

at Fairfield, nobody takes
any notice. Only when

a can is shaken do we lift
or turn our heads to look

to where the noise is coming
from. Graffiti is writ

then erased by the spray
filling the plastic bags.

Hey, this ain't America, man,
I say to myself. This

is another country, mate.
We do things differently here.

This is Friday
24/03/1995.

This is the 2.07
to Hurstbridge.

At the next station
they get off the train

without having looked at anyone,
without having spoken.

Some shift in their seats,
slowly shaking their heads

in disbelief. Then there are those
who seem to have lost

their place on the page
of the book they are reading.

Comfortable in the knowledge
that the train is not going

to derail, other passengers continue
to sleep or stare into space –

and the silence is killing.

Café society

for Craig

Back then there was no need to look.
We knew what was written on the blackboard.
The menu never changed:
Spaghetti, fettucine, and pasta of the day.
On Friday the pasta of the day was gnocchi.
We always ordered gnocchi and two glasses of cleanskin red,
Then began to talk music, football, politics, and poetry.
We have been doing this for more than twenty years.
Today the tradition continues.

Since last Friday our teams have won and lost,
There has been a change of government,
You have released a new CD, and I
Have made more amendments to my manuscript.

Sometimes we get lucky and find a table,
But more often than not we end up sitting on
The stools along the dark timber panel wall
Where the quasi-quattrocento mural
Has been replaced by scenes of still life.
I remember when people shared a table with strangers
Before another bar and bench with mirrors was built.
Either you or I once said the two things were unrelated,
While the other thought it was symptomatic
Of a more widespread malaise in our society.
Over bowls of pasta we lament the changes
To the menu, the liberal increase in prices…
The fact our favourite waiter is gone.

You return to the table with two coffees,
Your tongue having tripped up on
The consonantal minefield of café latte.
In these moments I imagine you on stage
Stammering through The Who's "My Generation".
Yet your stutter disappears when you sing.
As does mine.
And when you begin to tell me of the ancient belief
That such afflictions were due to the gods
Attempting to speak through the mouths of mortals
We both laugh and agree the gods can only say so much.

Over the years flashier brasseries and bars
Have opened (and closed) in the city's numerous lanes and alleyways,
But we find we prefer the familiarity which breeds content.
We step out onto the street and, before going our different ways
(You toward Parliament House, me to the bookshop),
Agree, as we do every Friday, to meet again the following week
And continue our conversation.

The dream

Our eyes follow the bulging hip
Of the not-so-handsome odalisque
To the clumsy hand and awkward feet
Which belie the artist's grasp of graphics.
We focus on the reclining woman
Because her presence is enigmatic;
But it's the figure of the charming native
(Half hidden in the paysage exotique)
And not the naked body of Yadwigha
Which makes the painting so hypnotic.
Et Rousseau? I'l s'est cache parmi l'herbe
Behind the red velvet chair playing the comic.
The foliage from a Paris street
He makes a forest of Afrique.
Bird beast and flower?
Pastiche of journals on the tropics.

Remembering Hiroshima

there was a flash like lightning
followed by a roaring silence
and a burst of heat upon the skin
then a barely audible 'boom'
like the sound of distant thunder
i remember waking from one dream
and walking into another
through the blue phosphorescent flames
which flickered like the reels of silent film
like insects trapped in amber the dead
embraced or sat silently at prayer
a woman with a hundred heads was eating air like mad
it was then that i turned away
from the ruins and went to the river
where an animal drifted downstream like an upturned table
so i took the table to ferry people across the river
here the dying would not look at the living
or those wanting to live
and wished that they were dead
while the living felt like dying
yet did not care for those about to die
black rain began to fall and the river forgot to flow
so i stepped off the table and walked across the water
in the distance i could see winged horses rising
from the pools of blood on the ground and seas
springing from the earth at the touch of their hooves

Obeying the call

Although the mind has gone to seed
The weathered hands and heart
Obey the call.

It must be hard to break a spell
Of sixty years; a ritual forged
By four generations of men

And borne by every father's son.
How else explain this strange behaviour
So early in the day?

This need to rise before the sun,
Tend the cows, turn the soil,
Or mend a fence

That used to be around here once.
Now, there are nurses to attend to him,
Take him back to bed,

Arrange it so that things return
To normal in this ward, adjust the sheets
To hold him firmly in his place.

THE BARRIER RANGE

2006

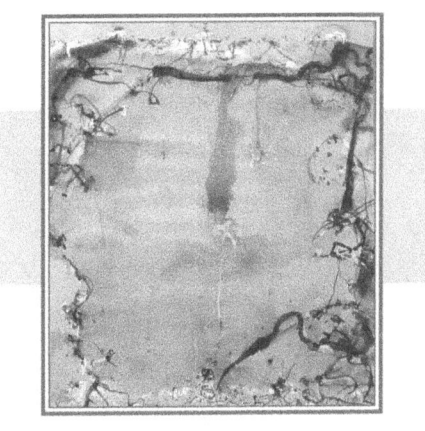

The Barrier Range
a journey to Broken Hill
Barbara Wills

Notes on *The Barrier Range*

Culturally appropriate terminology and language

As a work of historical fiction, *The Barrier Range* is redolent of a different era, having been first published in 2006. Some of the language is outdated and inappropriate to First Nations people, such as the disrespectful term 'Aborigine/s', which is used to refer to Aboriginal people/s. This term endures as an historical artefact, as do derogatory terms such as 'black/s' and 'native/s'.

Draft of Letter to Mr. John Macadam, Honorary Secretary, Exploration Committee, Royal Society of Victoria

3rd July 1860

Dear Mr. Macadam
Secretary 'The Expedition'

Having heard from Newspapers that you are seeking Assistants to accompany the main Party to the Interior on an Exploring Expedition, I wish to make myself available for appointment.

Although I have lived in the Colony all my life, I do not as yet know how to climb a Gum Tree a l' Aboriginee & drag or cut out an Oppossum. Nor am I used to groom Horses, to cook, & to serve at table. However, while my exploration has been restricted to Bushing-Parties around the Settlement I am receptive to receiving Tuition in the Art of taking lunars to improve my astral navigational skills. I also have an Uncle who worked at 'Killingsworth' near Yea before moving to Adelaide. He now lives in Broken Hill, and he would often relate to me Stories about the Outback before I lost contact with him. However, I recently received a Letter from my Uncle in which he stated that he was again desirous of making my acquaintance. Nevertheless, I do not think it matters about much Bush Experience because the Committee has appointed Police Superintendent Robert O'Hara Burke as Leader of the Exploration Expedition, & I read in the Newspaper that on the Goldfields he once got lost on a well marked track from Yackandandah to Beechworth.

Whilst Mr. Burke's Hygiene cannot be questioned (his Habit of bathing for Hours in an outdoor Tub wearing nothing but his Police Helmet are Legendary) I believe he may lack the necessary Organisational Skills to keep an accurate Record of the Journey to the Interior. The Press reported they had found a Note on the Wall of his Beechworth House which said: 'You are requested not to read anything on these walls. I cannot keep any record in a systematic manner, so I just jot down things like this.' I therefore believe my Experience in Journalism will be of a Benefit to the Party and to the Society.

Although I am, like Don Quixote, 'verging on Fifty,' I believe I have great powers of Physical Endurance & am in Robust Health. I can obtain for you Certificate of Good Character as Sober, Honest & Industrious Person. I know that Ludwig Becker, Artist & Geologist, is over Fifty Years Old so I do not think my Age & lack of Experience in the Bush Life is important.

I believe that what I lack in Experience & Social Connections I make up for with Enthusiasm. Unlike Charles Dickens, who in his new Book, 'A Tale of Two Cities,' says: 'It was the best of times, it was the worst of times,' I rather like to think these are the most exciting of times. I have just finished reading 'On the Origin of the Species by Means of Natural Selection, or the Preservation of Favoured Species in the Struggle for Life' by Charles Darwin, and I have come to the conclusion that the Interior of Australia may hold the Key to the Knowledge of the Origin of the Universe. The Explorer, George Grey, has seen Strange Creatures drawn in Caves by Aboriginees & has said that 'the natives of Australia are generally fond of narrating tales of fabulous and extraordinary animals, such as gigantic snakes.' I also saw on the Television that there are Reports of a large Serpent with the Colors of the Rainbow living on an Inland Sea in the Centre of Australia.

While I am not a Member of the Melbourne Club, I do, for what it may be worth, wish to advise you that I am a Member of the Geelong Football Club. (Indeed, it would be a Thrill & a Privilege to pass through Mirrool in the Riverina on the way to the Gulf & see the Wheat Silo over which Billy Brownless kicked a Football in his bare Feet). I also Hunt & Shoot with the Austin Family at Barwon Park who have recently introduced into Australia a Superior Breed of Rabbit from England for the purposes of the Sport of Shooting.

As the Committee can see, it is my Love of Adventure, and the Desire to Record for Posterity the Achievements of this Expedition, which compels me to apply to be a Member of the Exploration Party. Just as I do not seek Land or Gold in the Colony, I do not want to Tame the Country, Classify its Species of Flora & Fauna, or Civilize its Sable Inhabitants. It is not for my own Fame or the Glory of God that drives me to Explore, but, like Ernest Giles, it is for the feeling of 'wild charm and exciting desire.' It is the Chance to Experience the 'different states of the brightest hope and the deepest misery.' (Leichhardt). It is to be a Journey of Discovery without Appropriation. A Journey to find my Uncle. To find Myself.

I have the Honor to be Sir
Your Humble & Obedient Servant

Ray Liversidge

Viva Victoria

Neumayer takes Burke to one side:
'Forget Crown casino and the Grand Prix,

this baby's costing £15,000 and is
going to put this colony on the map.

We may be the new kid on the block
at the moment, Burke, but when you return

they'll be calling us the biggest and best.'

'Picturesque confusion'

Royal Park's packed like
the MCG on Grand Final day.

I call to Becker that it looks like
half the colony's here to wish us luck.

'I think we'll need it,' he yells back,
trying his best to stay balanced

while holding on tight to his sketch book.

The weather

Burke brings his horse alongside Landells.
'What's the weather like up there?' he asks.

'Get stuffed!' says Landells, tugging on
the rein. The camel spits on the dirt,

farts into a warm nor'-wester.

Cheer, boys, cheer

At 3.45 pm we leave Royal Park
already running three hours late –

the music of the band and the cheering
behind us now as we move

out past the stone cairn
and onto Sydney Road

on route to the village of Essendon
and the unknown...

Stuck in the middle

I'm standing in the middle
of the road helping Brahe

pick up busted bags
of flour and sugar

when Landells trots by
on his camel.
'What the fuck!..'

'The wheels of the wagon
got stuck in the tracks, sir,

and before you could say
'cheer, boys, cheer,'

we get rammed up the arse
by a No. 19 tram.'

From green to red

We follow
Calder Highway
to Bendigo
and onto the Terrick-Terrick plains
From the green
of cedars and ferns
to mulga   saltbush   red earth

Finding myself

I find myself
on an arid plain

looking at elders
from Wadi Wadi

History

In 1824 Hume & Hovell discovered
a river south of the Murrumbidgee

They called it the Hume

Four years later Sturt sailed the Murrumbidgee
down to the Hume and renamed

this *broad and noble river* the Murray

History (take two)

Ngurunderi chuckum spear
nothing kill'm Pondi

Pondi bin go more far
this way   that way

make 'im water long way
bye and bye Dhungulla[1]

---
[1] Dhungulla is the Ngarrindjeri word for Murray River

Finding myself again

I find myself in a Becker water-colour
looking at elders from Wadi Wadi

standing on the other bank amongst
red river gums. Some are naked,

others wearing animal skins
or the clothes of Europeans
Then a group in Land Rights
T-shirts outside a tent embassy

with clenched fists and black armbands

Cry me a river

The river is within us, the sea is all about us
- T.S. Eliot

This is not the river
I stepped in over

60 million years ago
or minutes since sleeping

This river is a different voice
which speaks to crops

and whose mouth is now closing

This river is a different god
a brown and brackish god
with blue-green algae

Salt is on the desert pea
Salt is in the gum tree

Catch of the day

No golden
    silver or
        Macquarie perch

No small
    hardy heads

No purple-
    spotted gudgeon

No trout
    or Murray cod

Just European carp
    kicking sand
        in the faces
            of native fish

The aesthetics of disappearance

All was uncertainty and conjecture in this region of magic
– Edward John Eyre

Leaving bitumen is
like forgetting words

of a favourite song
or lines of a familiar poem.

Off the road my mind
Deconstructs the clutter

of creature comforts and sings
into existence a foreign landscape

of Spinifex sand and gibbers.

Purple haze

Nothing between
land and above

but lines of saltbush
in a blue-green

(almost purple) haze

now 'scuse me
while I kiss the sky

The orange tree

I turn off
the dirt road

stop the engine
and sit out

the dust storm
in silence

my only correspondence
burning saltbush

You've got mail

When the party reach the pub at dusk
the publican has a beer waiting.

'Heard you blokes was comin'.'

'How did you know that?' Wills asks.

'Bush telegraph.'

Green sticks

'So, where you blokes headin'?'
says Tom, wiping the bar.

'Up to the Gulf,' says Burke.

Outside, the waterbirds could be heard
settling on the lake.
'We're going to be the first to cross
this continent from south to north.'
'Any of you been in the desert before?'
Tom asks with a grin.

'Not the desert as such,' says Wills.

A local sitting at the bar
tugs at his cabbage-tree hat.

'Green sticks,' he says, leaning
forward and sniggering in his glass.

'Stupid fuckin' green sticks.'

Just passing through

'Get many people staying here?'
I ask, looking out on the near-empty carpark.

'Nah. Laidleys Ponds's a pretty quiet place.
Mostly land speculators lookin' for sheep

and cattle runs, and claypan squatters.
Most folk go to Willyama, nor-west of 'ere.

Matterfact, 'ad a bloke in 'ere
only yesterdee askin' directions.

Come up from Adelaide, up th' other
Side of th' river from you mob.'

Burke lifts his weary head.
'His name wasn't Stuart, was it?'

Tom pours another round
Before answering.
'Nah. Sumthin' like that though.
Sturt. That's it. Charlie Sturt.

Said 'e was goin' to th' centre
to find an inland sea.'

Up the creek

'Another beer fellas?' asks Tom.

'No thanks. I think we'll retire
to our rooms for the evening.

Got to prepare for an early start
in the morning,' says Burke.

'Just stayin' th' one night are ya?'

'Yes. We'll rest for a couple of days
further up the creek, then head north.'

'Know where ya goin' then?'

'Wil, here, is the surveyor. He'll show
us the way.' Burke says, moving off his stool.

'Ya got two chances of findin' water
with a compass, mate – Buckley's or none.'

Just the bloke

'Can you tell us where there's water?'

'No. But I do know just the bloke.'

'Bill Wright's 'is name. Managed
th' cattle station Kinchega for three years
before John Baker sold it.
Says he's lookin' for a job.'

Burke watches as the publican
Hangs a sign over the bar.

Burke & Wills
Slept Here

'As good as any tracker our Bill is.
Knows every water hole north of 'ere

to th' Cooper. Even got a creek
named after 'imself at Bulloo.'

Photo opportunity

At Pamamaroo I watch the sun
setting over the Menindee Lakes.

All is silent except for
the occasional clicking of cameras.

Pelicans glide over dead trees and settle
on the dark water looking for fish.
Herons and cormorants in overcoats of grey
and black patrol the shores like soldiers.

'It's hard to imagine there's a shortage
of water beyond this point,' Burke says, as if to himself.

My eye follows the pipeline
that runs to Broken Hill…

and I wonder how Sturt's getting on.

Nothing but about the boat

'He fancies we shall soon come upon
the great waters of the interior,' Brock says,

fixing me with a stare.
'Nothing is heard but about the boat.

It's giving me the shits.'

Desert calenture

Sturt stops Duncan,
stands high in the stirrups,

and stares out at another
plain in front of him.

'I have ordered Morgan
to prepare and paint the boat,'

he says to me, looking like
he's about to jump from the saddle.

'We must be ready, Ray,
for flood or field.'

Bullocks

Let us steer to the Northward, comrades!
To the Bush with her witching spells;
To the sun-bright days and the camp-fire blaze
And the chime of the bullock bells!

– Beyond the Barrier, Will Ogilvie

across
    sandy
        ridges

drays
    sway

like
    drunken
        boats
each
    load
        lurching

through
    stunted
        cypress

acaciae
    atriplex
and
    the bullocks'
        necks

bloodied
    at the yoke

Aquatic similes

In moments of poetic confusion
Sturt writes of sand ridges

succeeding each other
like the waves of the sea,

only to have them solidify
and terminate on the plain

like so many headlands
projecting into the sea.

Plain prose

I fear it is doubt and not the heat
which dispels the dream

of an inland sea and convinces Sturt
to dispense with aquatic similes

as he dryly observes 'that all the water
seen glittering on the plain has disappeared.'

Drought

The sky is blue astonishment, a seamless packed blue
blue hordes arriving billion-fold from all directions
with bursting cases
– Philip Salom

I can do
   nothing
      but watch
  budgerigars

    abandon
        the big top
          of blue
        to look for
         rockpools

leaving
    nankeen plovers
      to somersault
        and tumble
      swoop
     and sway
       on thermal
     swings
as I swoon
       and drift...

Landscape and language

Vowels like water, consonants like rock
– Howard Nemerov

So, what to make of this country?
Is it not to be understood, as Sturt said?

Are we to be seduced by budding shrub
and wildflower purpler than the prose of Giles,

only to be taken for a long reconnoitring ride,
like Leichhardt, around a river bend

and onto an unbegotten plain where there are
no vwls lk wtr, cnsnnts lk rck?

Hill of mullock

'I was of the opinion, my dear fellow,
that no gold would be found in "them
thar hills" as the colloquial saying goes.
However, I was hopeful of finding tin
and silver in that particular region
referred to with scant and mock
regard by those myopic miners from
Silverton as the "hill of mullock".'

My eyes follow Rasp's outstretched finger
over the saltbush plain, tents and shanties,
past ragged children playing skittles in
the dirt, beyond airborne spinning pennies
of the two-up school to the dark hill flawed
like an old and broken blunt toothed saw.

Dark satanic mills

Dear Craig,

Included in this letter is my fourth article. It's taken a while but I have finally made it to Broken Hill. As I mention in my report the locals seem to have more of an affinity with South Australia than their own State. You may recall that when the Adelaide Crows won the Premiership in 97 (and 19bloody8!) there was TV vision of the players visiting here. I bet if the Swans ever win the flag they would never travel further west of Sydney than Parramatta! And who could blame them if they didn't want to come here. This town is hell on earth! Picture a place between Blake's dark satanic mills and an American wild west town and you've got it.

Speaking of the American wild west, I've been reading some more dime novels. It's interesting how frontiersmen like Wild Bill Hickok and Kit Carson have already been popularised as western heroes. In fact, the American west is anything but wild these days. The Native Americans have been all but dispossessed of their tribal areas as settlers continue with their inexorable search for land. Buffalo Bill has turned the Plains conflict with the Native Americans into a travelling sideshow called the 'Wild West Show'. Even the great Apache chief, Geronimo, was turned into a circus attraction. For four months he toured with Buffalo Bill's troupe, where he received $50 a week and was expected to sign autographs for the beguiled audience. While the cowboys have been made larger than life, the Sioux chiefs Crazy Horse and Sitting Bull have been killed and forgotten. Here, a similar thing is happening. Yet, how do we compensate the Aborigines for their loss of life and land? Why, issue them with blankets to celebrate the Queen's birthday, that's how! I don't think it's a coincidence that only a week after this Govt. gesture the phrase 'White Australia' appeared in a new Brisbane weekly newspaper, the Boomerang. But I digress. Let me bring you back to this wild west NSW town!

Remember the huge brickfielder that dumped Mallee dust on Melbourne in 83? Well, you ain't seen nothin' (and you don't see nothin'!) like the dust storms that regularly blow through here. Then, if it's not the dust getting into your eyes and lungs, it's the noxious fumes from the numerous smokestacks. The Greenhouse Effect is nothing new, my friend. I read in the Barrier Truth that the Statue of Liberty has just been unveiled in New York. I think the lines 'Give me your tired, your poor / Your huddled masses yearning to breathe free' could apply to people here.

While good money can be made by underground miners, the majority of the workers are poorly paid and work in atrocious conditions. The real winners are the shareholders, especially those with BHP stock. The town is rife with speculation of a mineral boom. In fact, I was in Argent St yesterday where they were openly trading shares off the back of carts. One bloke told me that Poseidon is going to be the next big thing so I bought a brick of shares just in case it comes off. As I was in a speculative mood I also put half a brick on Mentor in the Melbourne Cup. The owner, Don Wallace, is a shareholder in BHP so most of the town has backed it.

A lot of the miners here have come from Silverton. In the space of 10 years Silverton went from a boom town to a ghost town, and is now a town dependant on the tourist dollar for its existence. In fact, you may be interested to know (I am sounding like a tourist, aren't I?) that Wake in Fright, Mad Max 2 and The Adventures of Priscilla: Queen of the Desert were filmed around the Silverton area.

Which brings me to my uncle. Did you know he was in Priscilla? If you look very closely at the pub scene, which was shot in the Palace Hotel where I'm staying, you can see his face in the background. The publican told me Ron (or Pat, as he is known here) used to be a regular, but he hasn't seen him for months. When I asked why everyone called my uncle Pat, he said that's just how it's always been. He suggested I visit the Lodges around town as Ron was a member of – check this out – the Royal Antediluvian Order of the Buffaloes. Phew! Unfortunately, none of his 'brothers' could, or would, enlighten me as to his whereabouts. It was the same story at the RSL. I just hope he's not a member of any of the other numerous friendly societies in this town! At one stage I was even going to look for him in a church. I was nearly out the door and into Argent Street when the boys at the bar broke into fits of laughter. Apparently, Ron would say he was 'going to church' whenever he intended going out for a beer.

At times I have felt like giving up, Craig, but after speaking to some locals I'm determined to find him. From what I have been told, my uncle has, like this part of the country, a harsh and ruddy complexion. And while many have walked over this land and dismissed it on appearances (without realising the wealth beneath the surface), I'm sure many people in the past have looked upon my uncle and been quick to judge him. The only way I'm going to be able to form an opinion is to locate him. This morning I heard reports that Sturt and his party have been stranded by drought near Milparinka. They have been unable to find any water in the nearby waterholes let alone locate an inland sea, yet Sturt remains optimistic about realising his dream. Like Sturt, I'm determined to continue the search.

I'll write again soon.

Best wishes

P.S. I'm glad I put my bet on yesterday because today, Melb. Cup day, there was a fire which destroyed most of Argent St. Understandably, people were more concerned with avoiding danger and helping put out the fire than worrying about the result of the Cup. The good news is that no lives were lost… and Mentor got up at 7/1. You fuckin' beauty!

Having travelled with Burke and Wills from Melbourne to Menindee, Ray Liversidge decided to go west (as any young man should) and join Charles Sturt in his search for an inland sea. He went so far west on the plains of New South Wales that he reached...

the edge of sundown

What's in a name? the bard asked. A rose by any other name etc. The Hill. That's what the locals call Broken Hill. Before that it was known as Silverfield because, like nearby Silverton, silver was found in the soil. To the Wiljakali tribe it has always been Willyama – an Aboriginal name for youth. Europeans originally called this area Willyama but changed the name in recognition of the only notable feature on the saltbush plains: a jagged rocky ridge.

That rocky ridge turned out to be a massive orebody containing the largest silver-lead-zinc mineral deposit in the world. Since Charles Rasp pegged out a 40 acre area on the five-mile-long line of lode many leases have been granted and many mining companies formed. Broken Hill Propriety Company Limited (BHP) is the biggest and has the best section of the outcropping orebody.

Manic mining activity has seen the razing of the jagged ridge, the sinking of deeper shafts, and the proliferation of blast furnaces and waste dumps.

What's in a name, indeed. This place by any name would smell as foul.

Standing in the middle of Argent Street it's hard to imagine that underneath my feet is the oldest rock formation in New South Wales. These rocks were formed about 1800 million years ago during the Precambrian age. Over the last 20 million years the uplifting along fault zones and changing weather conditions produced the land formation which Charles Sturt has called Stanley Barrier Range, in honour of the British Secretary of State for the Colonies. The area is now known as the Barrier Range.

A politician from Sydney once referred to Broken Hill

as the 'edge of sundown' because it was so far west of the capital city. Walter Sully, owner of the merchant store, Sully Emporium, says such a remark is typical of the contemptuous attitude of the NSW Government toward the town.

'From day one they've done nothing for us. Out of sight, out of mind is the way they think,' Walter said.

The feeling against the State Government is so strong that some people in the community are calling for a secession from NSW and the formation of a new State to be called Centralia.

Walter Sully speaks for most businesses when he says: 'I do most of my trade with Adelaide. The mines do, too. I'm small bickies, but with the mines we're talking big business.'

When the State Government refused to support the development of the town, Broken Hill looked to the east. The South Australian Government agreed to extend its railway to Cockburn on the SA/NSW border. A private railway company, the Silverton Tramway Company, was formed and connection made to Silverton. When the mining boom in Silverton went bust the line was taken to Broken Hill. Smelters were built at Port Adelaide and Port Pirie, and ore sent there for treatment and export. This commercial link with South Australia had a significant effect on the milieu of Broken Hill. While remoteness has produced a spirited independence in this close-knit community, the link with the east has eased the feeling of isolation. Locals even set their clocks by South Australian time.

When graziers moved into this area with their sheep and cattle they destroyed what vegetation existed. Any grass and shrub left was finished off by rampant rabbits and wild goats. Trees were felled to build mines and smelters, and for household firewood. The houses – or tinnies as they are called – don't have nature strips or back yard lawns. Everything here is red dirt, and because of the lack of vegetation and rain (less than 10' a year) the dirt is quickly reduced to dust.

The local paper, *Barrier Truth*, describes the dust as an unwelcome suitor: '*Broken*

Hill dust has an insidious way of penetrating and exploring one's anatomy. It clings to you and nothing but soap plentifully applied will disencumber you from its embrace.' Applying the soap is one thing, however, working up a lather is another. Due to drought, small rainfall and inadequate town planning, Broken Hill finds itself with a hazardous shortage of water. Water is so scarce and expensive that miners often go for several days without washing themselves. Taking a shower might cost 1s 3d, or about one eighth of a labourer's daily wage.

Only after two years of vehement public protests did the Government pass an Act enabling a private company to supply water to the district. Unfortunately, that legislation came too late for 128 people who died of typhoid. While Broken Hill gets about a quarter of Sydney's average rainfall, its mortality rate is twice the State average.

Early settlement problems, however, did not stop the influx of people. Men came in their thousands from the goldfields of Victoria, the copper mines of South Australia, and even the tin and copper mines in Cornwall, England to work in this mining town.

Mining, by its very nature, attracts the itinerant. Feverish activity often means that minerals are quickly exhausted, and so the miner moves on in search of the next strike. The landscape is already dotted with abandoned shafts and deserted towns. However, things in Broken Hill appear to be different.

In its first three years the settlement of Broken Hill went from a tent and shanty town of a few hundred people to a municipality with a population of 11000. Timber and corrugated iron buildings soon replaced tents and cabins. Another three years on and many of those buildings are being rebuilt in brick and stone. The population has nearly doubled, making Broken Hill the third largest town in NSW. Suddenly, many thousands of people are viewing Broken Hill as a more permanent place of residence. Like a rose, the Hill continues to bloom and smell attractive to the locals.

Diary entry

8th April 1889

Met a few locals today and asked what they did for entertainment in this town. Told me nothing happens until Saturday night when everyone 'goes down Argent Street' to hear a band play or see a picture at Bert Sayer's Skating Rink. Even though it's my birthday I decide to stay in my hotel room and listen to 'Books and Writing' on Radio National. They review these latest books:

Des Kapital by Karl Marx

Germinal by Emile Zola

Une Saison en enfer by Arthur Rimbaud

On wall is a print of Van Gogh's painting of a poor Flemish mining family, *The Potato Eaters*. As I go to turn off light I notice kerosene lamp is just like one in painting. Is all of this coincidence, serendipity or synchronicity? Tomorrow I'm going to look for a job in mines to find out.

Deconstructing a bridge

Think big. Picture the Sydney
Harbour Bridge spanning five miles,

Flexing a mile upward. Imagine it
Is a solid silver-lead-zinc line of

Lode in metamorphic rock with an
Outcropping arch of oxidised ore.

Visualize thousands of men in soot
(Visualize a boardroom with men in suits)

Dismantling a mountain by sharing hands
(Dismantling a mountain by handling shares)
In a time incommensurable
With the cycle it took to form.

Pecking order

At first light we gather like fledglings
outside the office of The Big Mine.

From behind the wire fence
the foreman appears, his finger

jabbing the heavy air like
a mantling cock at mating time.

'You You You You And…
you,' he says, looking me in the eye.

From somewhere in the line there's
a shuffle of feet, then a flurry of words:

'Hey, this ain't no 'On the Waterfront,' mate.'
The counterpunch is quick and final:

'And you ain't no contender.
Now get outta here, ya bum.'

Picture postcard perfect

The camera pans the landscape
like an eye following Rasp's finger
to the hill of mullock. Click.

> Suspended above the broken back of
> the outcrop, flying foxes and uplifted picks.

Pull back from the open cut,
the smokestacks, smelters and magnetic
mills to the foreground. Click.
> Small and heavy sacks of ore hand-sorted,
> knapped, bagged and stacked on bullock carts.

Leave the bullocks and follow the sweep
of the wooden viaduct past the waste dumps
and focus on Delprat Shaft. Click.

Underground

At the
foot of

the poppet
head to Delprat

Shaft we assemble
like lost souls and
wait for the cage to
take us underground

Four bells

I might be back in Melbourne
taking an elevator to the office

except my world has turned
upside down   descending a shaft

to darkness   the number of bells
tolling the depth of its destination

Truckin' or skimpin'

'You can either work truckin' or
skimpin'. Either pushin' trucks of ore

from the shute to the shaft, or takin'
skimps of waste from the shaft and

fillin' in the stopes. The pay's the same:
8s. 4d. for an 8 hour day, 10 bob a shift
for you skilled blokes. Twenty
minutes to eat your crib. Any questions?'

I stand in the plat with the other men
blinking into the blackness. Nobody speaks.

The manager issues a warning with
the three candles and iron spider:

'If I find out any of you blokes are
sundowners and don't know a pick from
a bloody shovel, you'll be back on a station
in no time fuckin' sheep for a quid a week.'

The creep

'Id'n't tew bad wunce y'd get used
t'th' dark. Pay's better'n

up t'grass, and tis a 'elluva lot cooler
'n summer down 'ere. An' th' good

thing is, y'don' 'ave Cap'n lookin'
orr y'sholda all th' time.

Bein' on tutwork means th' more
yew d'do th' more yew'd get'.
Five minutes past crib time, half-
listening to Pat the Cornish miner,

imagining the two of us sitting in
Trafalgar Square feeding scraps to pigeons.

'They wun't 'urt 'ee, lad. 'Tis when
y'dun't see 'um that y'oum gotta wurry.'

Another crust of bread hits the dust.
Another rat scurries out of the shadows.

Survival, Pat says, requires rat cunning,
your wits about you, listening for

creaking timber, the ground to speak, the creep.

Exceeding the speed limit

Pat tells the story of
the day the earth coughed.

How twenty men were
Working in the South Mine

When told to leave the stope
And move to the storey below.

Walking from the tunnel and away
From danger the miners welcomed

the chance to rest and clear
their throats of dirt and fog.

When the lungs of the earth collapsed
a whoop of air went like a wave...
and lifted off their feet like feathers
nine men death-sped to the wall.

Working on a chain-gang

I hold the steel,
Pat hits it with
a hammer. A quarter
turn, another blow.
And so it goes:
hammer & tap
hammer & tap
until the hole is drilled.
The face is fired,
the roof barred down,
the fallen rock popped

with a sprawler.
And so it goes:
blast & pop
blast & pop
until the ore is carted.

And so it goes:
hammer & tap
blast & pop
until the shift is over.

The big O

'No man can strike'

I wanna kill him

'a drill and sing'

but I know it

'at the same time'
wouldn't be right

'now get to work.'

So, between the flickering
And gutter of the candle,

I see the boss is right.
As of today there will be

no more workin' for The Mine.

Acedia

A chthonic mountain of my own making,
the fourth storey reboant with doing:

an Italian poet's quid pro quo
for a life of indolence, a failure of love.

Leave your candle and drill,
the voice says. Take the cage to daylight,

find the Virgil to your Dante.

Mutawintji

1.

carrying the bad poetry
of Giles in my head

> *be bold of heart*

and my uncle's letters in my hand

> *be strong of will*

I follow the dry creek bed
of the sandstone gorge
and stop at a rockpool

> *My Tung is stkig to my mouth*

to refill my drink bottle

> *My ey Dassels*

and move out of the sun
to the shade of a shallow cave

2.

and still the *celestial sounds continue...*
dispensing melody and pain

> *be bold of heart*

the letters remain

> *be strong of will*

on my lap unread

3.

a shadow
   falls across
     my knees

above the ridge
   of the Byngnano Range
     a swallow circles
       the setting sun

like a bent finger
   around a skull

4.

in the silent scream of the cave mouth
is it the ripping yarns about savages

and human sacrifice or the incantations
of sacred ceremonies of initiation

which makes me turn around?

in the dying light the wall throws up
as many questions as answers

is it blood or is it ochre
on that red right hand?

5.

a play of light
   upon the wall?
      fingers moving?...

     *

a rockspider sidles from the shadows
    stops   spreads its legs
  and flattens its body against the boulder

*

a yellow-footed rock wallaby
  suddenly lifts its head
    as if sensing a stranger
then stands erect
  on the darkening plain
    and stares at the candlelit cave
      in the distance

*

  nightfall

warm air nasalflare of flora
    fuchsia
      emu bush
        honey of the eucalypt
  fauna pawpad mouthgnaw clawscratch
    creaturecrawl
      a squall of insects
        and skytrawling birds following

an indrawn breath

      the shuffle of papers

*

...as if the pain came
  suddenly
    and out of the blue
the words written
    quickly
  on scraps of paper
  bits of cardboard

    the back of cereal packets
love's *disjecta membra*

        *

the tortured scribblings
   like traceries of insects
      in the dirt

       *

her letters to you
   as sweet and lethal
      as sugar

      *

Dearest Darling Pat,

(Hello)

I'm sure you must be surprise to received this letter. Well, my name is _____. I'm 35 years old and I got three children. Its very hard for me to look after the children because I got no house and anything here I pay 180 dollar's for the Rent and to pay the scool fees and to buy things so its very hard.

      *

her given name
   a palindrome
her surname
   one letter shy
      of being a devil

      *

nearly twice her age
   and twice as gullible
as far away as Fiji
   she could see you coming

*

she has seen the photo
    you sent her
  (the one she kisses *all the time*)
now she wants to *see you from my eye's*
   so we can enjoy ourself very nicly
   never mind you got one leg or not
because she has *got*
 feelings for you darling
in fact *just think how much*
  she loves *you darling*
why you *can do everything*
 if *you (k)now darling*
  what she means
oh yes she needs you
   very very urgently

how can you resist her?

*

Red Red apple
Good for eating
you my Darling
Good for Kissing

*

within a month
  of her first letter
    you marry
at the ceremony
  when you *turned*
    to kiss her
      she was gone

*

> after three days
>> you return
>>> to Broken Hill

>> alone

Diary entry

1ˢᵗ March 1861

Arrived in Tibooburra after stay at Mutawintje where I read Ron's letters, etc. Very painful reading. His bitter experience certainly gives credence to cliche that love is blind. He hurt lots of people early in his life, then got hurt himself. That can be 'life' I suppose, but it certainly has made me regret how I've treated those close to me – friends, family, lovers... At end I think he was trying to seek forgiveness and find calm in his life. From papers I've read it was evident he was making plans to put his house on market and move down to Melbourne to be near me and my father. Unfortunately, he ran out of time.

My time in desert has certainly given me chance to think about things. At times the monotony and intractability of landscape ensures that the mind, as Giles says, 'is forced back upon itself' because the very isolation of environment renders you unprotected from inner voices. Yet *the immensity and antiquity of the desert both repel and fascinate. Like other forms of the sublime, the desert lures people towards the eroticism of death.* However, I must be wary of this self-absorption.

I know north is not way home, but have this strong feeling that Ron would want me to join Burke & Wills for final leg of their (and my) journey back home. Virgil left Dante at end of journey through Purgatory and put him in hands (oh how Dante wished it was into the arms) of Beatrice for his entrance to Paradise. Ron has gone, but his spirit is still there. But is it his spirit or is it new me? I tried to turn Ron into something he wasn't, yet he's still been able to change (or is changing) me. Who will be my Beatrice on final leg of journey? And is my trip a Divine Comedy in reverse? Am I heading into hell instead of heaven? Into damnation rather than grace? I only know I cannot will it – there has to be a preparedness for acceptance, a granting of humility.

Have been offered lift tomorrow from a miner who is heading up through channel country to Mt. Isa. Said he should be able to pick up trail of B&W. Publican filled me in with what's been happening with exploration party since they left Menindee back in Oct. last year, as there's been no shortage of coverage in papers and on TV. Too late to do an article for paper, but will record events in case I do article later or story.

No news is not good news

Burke and the boys
seem pleased to see me.

'Do you bring good
news from Cooper's Creek?'

Gray and King
return to jerking meat,

Burke tries to crack hardy,
while Wills looks down

at the toes protruding
from his Blunstones

when I tell them no.

Camping out

We move
　slowly
　　along the
　　　bends of
　the creek
　　by moonlight
numbering
　and naming
　　our camps:
Humid

　　　Muddy

　　　　　Mosquito.

Each day our daily bread

Although each man is given
a daily ration of twelve sticks

of meat and a quarter pound of flour,
for Gray it's not enough.

At Native Dog camp while dreaming
of a counter-meal at the Lake Boga Hotel

he is seen by Wills behind a tree
eating skilligolee and given a good thrashing

by Burke for his trouble.

Gammoning

Gray is penitent, Burke impatient.
That's no surprise – it's in his nature.

Yet, everyone can see Charlie's sick and weak.

Still Wills, fair Wills, even Wills believes

Gray gammoned he could not walk.

Ship of the desert

Wasted by dysentery and racked with cramp
Gray has to be strapped to a camel.

I wonder if he sees the irony in an old
sailor being lashed to a 'ship of the desert'.
I needn't worry. By the time we reach
Polygonum Swamp he is dead.

Not shamming

We take a day to bury Gray.
Burke helps lower the body into

the grave but stays untouched by death.
Meanwhile, grief works on Wills

for he now believes poor Gray
must have suffered very much

and regrets he thought him shamming.

Depot LXV

By moonlight Burke swears he sees
the camp of Brahe& Co.

Hope strengthens his legs as he stands
in the stirrups and cooees up the creek.

The shadows of trees quake and fall
across our path like folding tents
as we near the depot. All is silent,
then I hear Wills say: 'King, they are gone!'

DIG tree

I double-check the date on my watch.
'But that's today,' I tell a disbelieving Burke.
Falling to his knees our leader pushes aside
the horse and camel shit and commences to

do what the carved trunk of the tree instructs:

DIG
3 FT. N.W.
APR. 21 1861

Message in a bottle

Burke ignores the cache of food
and taking the papers out of the bottle,

asked each of us whether we were
able to proceed up the creek in pursuit

of the party. We said not.

If only

If only Wright had not waited so long in Menindee to leave for Cooper's Creek.

If only Brahe had waited one more day – what's one more when you've already waited 127 days?!

If only it was not true – as Brahe had said – that his party was in good health, then we might have followed them immediately to the Darling.

If only Gray had not died.
If only we had not taken a day to bury him.

If only...

Rage against the non-appearance of a *deus ex machina*

Both Burke and Wills with quills in hand
are the gentlemanly calm before my storm.

'Greatly disappointed at finding
the party here gone', scribbles Burke.

And Wills, as if looking over the shoulder
of his leader, writes of the disappointment

at finding the depot deserted...
My scream disperses the slumbering birds.

Bookings not essential

'I am Mr. Burke and these three gentlemen are members of my party. At this moment we are particularly famished and would welcome the opportunity of experiencing the varied, and undoubtedly excellent, cuisine of your most reputable dining establishment.'

The Yandruwandha stare at the four strangers.

'I must apologise for our somewhat dishevelled appearance and do, of course, realise that a hybrid uniform of flannel and horse blanket may not necessarily meet your dress standards. However, my colleagues and I would be most grateful if you could, for this one occasion, see fit to waive your formal attire requirements.

The Yandruwandha are unmoved.
'Perhaps my failure to make a reservation has led to confusion. I can explain. Of late, my men and I have been concentrating all our efforts on survival with the intention of reaching civilisation and... oh fuck it! Just show us to a table.'

What do you feel like?

Brahe: I'm so hungry I could eat a horse.

Wills: I'm sick of horse – I think I'll try the rat.

Cooper's Creek Cafe

Menu

Entree

Braised pheasant
('All feathers and claws' – William Wills)

Cutlet of yellow-bellied black snake cooked in its own juices
(Gave Burke a dose of dysentery)

Main Course

Rats baked in their skins with portulac herb
('Most delicious' – William Wills)

Camel casserole
('Like a carpenter's glue-pot' – Peter Warburton)

Fillet of horse meat with date sauce
('Healthy and tender' – William Wills)

Dessert

Nardoo muffin
('If you know where to look' – Anonymous)

Check out at the lights, man

For a week we live like, and with, the blacks.
They gave us food and offered their women

in exchange for sugar and fishhooks.
We took the food... and take our minds

off sex and death by chewing on pituri.
Around the fire that night the stars

never seemed so bright or life so funny
as when Wills giggled and said:

'I feel quite happy and perfectly
indifferent about my position.'

A bummer

coming
  down
as the sun
  comes up
only
  to find
the natives
  gone

Backtracking

We follow
their tracks
but fear

the blacks
have run
off into
the desert
like surface
water.

Burke
backtracks
on the Cooper –
and on the thought
of living like blacks –
and tries again to find
the South Australia border
and the mountain named Hopeless.

What the dickens

We cannot go on like this –
but we do go on like this.

There is nothing else to do
but to go on like this:

Burke and King up the creek
to look for the blacks,

Wills and I at home
discussing Charles Dickens.

A tale of two parties

Wills is worried; not about dying,
but the whereabouts of Burke and King.

In this tale of two parties he fears
they may be having the worst of times.

Yet I know things are no better 'at home'
when Wills disturbs me at my writing

to ask if I can take his watch
and a letter from his waistcoat pocket

with a promise to give them to his father.

What's in a name?

King returns – and fears I may be mad.
'It hasn't got the same ring about it, John.

Liversidge and King, King and Liversidge.
It's not like Laurel and Hardy,' I say,

laughing at the absurd theatre.
'Or even Burke and Wills.'

'No,' King says, helping me
make a mound of sand and rushes.

'No, it hasn't – and we're not dead, yet.'

Pie in the sky

I am not mad. King, too, sees it.
He has already shot one, and I

am keen to kill another before dusk.
'Look, John,' I say, pointing

to the branches of a towering eucalypt.
'A hawk or crow?' he asks, raising his gun.

'Neither. It's a boat.'

Unburied as I lie

'Why didn't you bury him, John?'
I ask, looking down at what might be

The body of a fallen soldier.
'It was Mr Burke's wish I place a pistol

in his right hand, and, as he said,
"leave me unburied as I lie".'

Empty gesture

'I know it is useless against a waddy
Or a spear, John, but if I were to die

I would like to be left unburied with
a pen, rather than a gun, in my hand.'

King, good naturedly, ridicules my request
for a theatrical end as we continue up
the creek to look for the Yandruwandha.

Empty-handed

We do not come with gifts,
yet they bring water and food

in coolamons and offer us
shelter in their gunyahs.

'Pirti-pirti sit down,' they say.
'Black fella puttem sleep spears long time.'

King nods his head, then says to me:
'We are welcome – and in no danger.'

Lost look about fella

I learn a little finger-yabber so to savvy,
but it is King who tries to explain

that the big talk fella are dead, and we
are lost look about fella who come

to ask to sit down long time all about
with the black fella until the white fella come.

Two fella dead, two fella live

'Find 'im whitefella – two fella dead –
bones belong 'im stink along bush –

two fella live little bit long way.'

Welch follows the two black boys and finds
a solitary figure in scarecrow rags
who throws up his hands at the sight of a white,
then falls on the ground in an attitude of prayer.
'Who in the name of wonder are you?'
Welsh asks the bedraggled figure.

'I am King, sir.'

Welsh turns to me. 'And you are...
er... Mr. Liversidge, I presume?'

TRIPTYCH POETS

2010

Triptych Poets

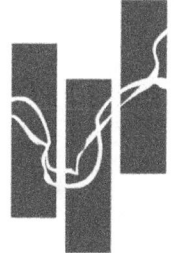

Ray Liversidge | Hilaire | Mary Mageau

Things to (and not to) do

A found poem from a notebook of Edna St Vincent Millay
(for Jordie Albiston)

Care for nothing except poetry.
Keep everything from mind but this.
Forget that *you* exist.

Even if suffering torment speak in voice
with *no hint* of pain. Keep corners
of mouth *up*. Cry as little as possible.

Disguise feelings when You-Know Who(m)
is in room. Have many lovers.
Remember things to do for Eugen.

Go out of doors every day. Putty
up holes where bees get into garage.
Put panes in several windows.

Exercise will-power in *all* things.
Have a drink, sometimes.
Never leave the syringe about.

Don't become sloppy in *anything*,
in thinking, in dress,
in *anything*. Don't fool yourself.

A corner store, another world

When the weather broke we were cubbyholed
in the house until the rain backed off.
Then, brushing aside the flywire screen, we scrambled
down the front steps and into the rain-swept street,
brother-lovingly launching our ice-cream sticks
on the gutter's exigent and spastic water.
Then, the winning was everything and nothing:
our splintered totems repeatedly slipping down
the drain mouth until we gave up the counting.
Returning to the neighbourhood, the street
seems smaller now – the cars and houses
tumescent with modernity. The sibling
bliss of musk sticks and sherbet bombs
a corner store – another world – away.

The baby and the bathwater

You said that if you did, you'd have to live
With it. The desire to harness the sun and wind
For power was everything: renewable energy
The alternative, the only answer. Coming from
Such a desolate place I was soon comfortable with
My heart's polarity, ready to be drawn to an open field
With you, exposed to all that the world could give.
But you wanted me earthed and, in the garden,
Turned, what was for you, true – not magnetic – north.
Then suddenly the weather changed: air filled with resistance:
And in those bleak and breathless moments following
You fell back on batteries and familiar habits –
All the while knowing I never was mechanically minded.
Right now I feel like a fossil fuelled by anger, baby,
A product passed its use by date. In the morning
I'll be poured out like used water… Then, like water,
Which always finds its level, settle, recycle.

The lawn

Spring has returned. The earth is like a child that knows poems.
– Rainer Maria Rilke

He is mowing the lawn, again.
Again it is unnecessary.
Like pulling grey hairs from
a greying head.
On another warm November evening
I put down the newspaper with
the interminable stories on emissions trading,
the growing number of climate change sceptics,
to watch him do what he does
every other Sunday:
go at it like there's no tomorrow.

I want him to stop
mowing the parched lawn,
but his body moves with such speed and purpose
that I fear he is afraid
of grass and its slow and chthonic growth.
I want him to take
the lawn clippings collected
(like analects) in the grass catcher,
and spread them at the foot of the tree
leaning into the corner of his garden.
I want to shake him
like the wind shakes his cottage garden
when it blows hot and hard
from the north.
I want him to enter
his house when he has finished
using the edge trimmer
and pick up a dictionary
and look up the word concinnity…
I need him to listen to the earth,
know poems.

Familial faces

A cloth collects dust best
I imagine her saying.
Better than a duster.
Her face one of several faces looking out of the frame
Of the photo I have lifted from the mantelpiece.
That face taken from this world many years ago,
And for years missing from my world,
But caught now – like the trophied fish we are holding –
In a black and white Kodak moment.

My mother and brother and sister, cousins, aunt, grandmother and I,
None of us were anglers.
Yet I remember how easy it was to catch flathead –
Letting the weight of the sinker take the line through fingers
And over the side of the boat until it found the ocean floor –
Then waiting in silence for a bite.
How quick and oft they took the hook!
And how frantically we yanked up the lines
And flung those fish into the boat
Where they flip-flopped for a while
Before resigning themselves to our fricative squeals and jibes
With quivering gill and unspeakable plosives.

And how easy and carefree those summers were,
How carefree and easy summers are when you're eleven or twelve.
How time moved metronomically, like the arm
On the dial of the Marshalite traffic signal
On Nepean Highway, Aspendale, in 1960 something.

And there is no end to remembering, yet only memory ends it.

Pockets swollen with stones and shells
His mother has chosen, he strolls the shore,
Heavy with the future:
The occasional whispers of siblings in his ear,
The grandmother gone with good riddance,
His cousins born from ghosts and becoming unworldly,
An aunt transported into the Hinterland.

The boy in the photo moves out of the frame
To the tea-tree cubby
Where a man brushes off sand clinging to his sunburnt skin.
The cubby is a cave: a hollow to hold the wind
Where no wind was.

A month of Sundays

Love, all alike, no season knowes, nor clyme,
Nor houres, dayes, moneths, which are the rags of time.
– John Donne

Today the world's contracted thus:
This bed – our centre – spread and fold.
Look how you eclipse the sun with a wink,
How I block out the moon with a nudge
From behind. O, such planetary joy
I haven't had since Copernicus was a boy!
Who knows what we are: that which is
Written in the stars; a postmodern text
Waiting to be read. Rain falls.
The morning passes unrehearsed.
The afternoon demands a script.
I suddenly think of something to do,
And you of doing something too… We both resist:
Our world replete with absolutely nothing,
Empty of the everydayness of everything.

Goya's Dog

You think: is it swimming or sinking?
You obey the dog blindly and mimic
Its movement. And you? You dust
For animal prints, suggest the 'lonely pooch'
Sleep outside its frame of reference.

You kennel the dog on a gallery wall.
You remember the dog from history.
You see the dog as something else.

Some do the things that doggies do,
Some, let slip the leash, wreak havoc,
Others remain impounded awaiting their release.
And you – dog's best friend – you paint the mongrel black,
Sling it a bone, turn a deaf ear to its howling.

The Divorce Papers

> *I see no sin:*
> *The wrong is mixed. In tragic life, God wot,*
> *No villain need be! Passions spin the plot:*
> *We are betrayed by what is false within.*
> – *Modern Love*, George Meredith

1. Eschatology

> *Sorrow/Is its own place*
> – *On a Deserted Shore*, Kathleen Raine

And that was all he could
remember of the night:

walking into the last
of the empty rooms,

looking out the window
at the white picket fence

and making a promise to
himself to fix the unhinged

latch on the front gate
first thing in the morning.

2. Hangover

I do not know myself without thee more.
– *Modern Love*, George Meredith

And like the times you had one glass too many
Your marriage didn't know when to stop.
For years you drift into unconsciousness
Then wake one morning with a hangover
To find the furniture and the children gone.
From habit you take two aspirin,
Surprising yourself with your circumspection.
You don't know whether to eat or not,
To sleep or stay awake –
And when wept-spent you want to rest
You find there is no peace, no quiet.

Your 'friends appear like paramedics'[2]
Administering advice on the therapeutic
Properties of Time. But for now there is no cure.
Somehow you go on: composing a villanelle
In Coff's Harbour on an autumn morning,
Reading at a Yarra Valley winery
Late one winter afternoon.

Every evening you return to a silent house,
Pour yourself a drink, allow ice to melt
As you would anger... Then wait for night to come,
For stars again to blink and break
Into countless shards of hardened light.

---

[2] From Andy Kissane's poem "Rising and Falling"

3. Bouquets

Happiness is not an ideal of reason but of imagination.
– Immanuel Kant

Bouquets are not cheap tricks.
Such gestures no sleight-of-
hand to make you reappear
to where you vanished from.
I cut you in half, he made you whole.
I'd do a David Copperfield
if it would bring you back again,
play Harry Houdini
if you would have me back again,
perform the sad clown routine
just to hear you laugh again.
Then when the crying's done
and love returns (as if by magic)
I promise to clean up my act
And never make you bend again
to smell the artificial flower on my lapel.

4. Envoi

In thy beauty is the dilemma of flutes.
– e e cummings

There are no love poems,
Only lyrics on love gone,
Or going, wrong. I know
No sonnets written in
Celebration of your beauty
(Just blank verses of cruelty)
No lines to your eyes,
Limericks to your lips,
Similes to liken you to
One thing or another.

These days I find myself
Lip syncing to songs about
Trying to lose those
I'm-losing-you blues.
The days write themselves.

5. Driving lesson

We wake in the same moment to ourselves and to things.
– Jacques Maritain

And, of course,
life goes on:
ignoring the signs,
indifferent to the stars,
deaf to the conspiratorial
whispering of the wind,
blind to the stranger
beckoning by the roadside,
declining the personal
invitations of each
and every roadside tree
to meet a woody end.

6. Half Moon Bay, Black Rock, Circa 1972

Every hair is numbered like every grain of sand.
– Bob Dylan

The signs were already there
If only we'd bothered to look:
'No Standing' on the road,
'No Boating' by the sea.
But desire knows no prophecy
Nor listens to rumours of rain.
Beneath the cliff face storied
With middens, mirror bush
Shimmering with water and moonlight,
We defied the weather and the gods.
I sat you on a blanket
And opened a book by Baudelaire.
I remember you asking what
Fleur de mal meant as I leant forward
And let down the dark tendrils of your hair.

Some thirty years later as I drive
Around Red Bluff I can feel the bay
Bending again to my will, see your face
Flashing past Rickett's Point
Like a stranger's on a reel of super 8,
Witness West Gate Bridge deconstructing,
Watch the waves retreating in slow
Motion to the Cerberus, and our love,
Like a breakwater, holding back the ocean.

7. Snapshots

Not sorrow breaks the heart
But an imagined joy
– On a Deserted Shore, Kathleen Raine

On those mornings you always seemed to wake before
The alarm, as if your biological clock was set to some
Troubled time that startled you from sleep
And started you on a chronological journey of grief.

Around every corner, along every road, down every highway
Every house you passed seemed blessed with domestic bliss,
Every room in every house holy with conjugal joy, every line
Of every love-gone-wrong song written just for you.

'Are we there yet?' You remember her tired attempts
To explain that desire can destroy any notion of distance
While imagining Lawson asking Wentworth the same question
And a gobsmacked Blaxland before mountains of blue.

And she – one of three sisters – turned to stone
Amongst Blue and Scribbly gums of the spur,
The Great Dividing Range a blur on the landscape,
The children like birds foraging in leaf litter at her feet.

Sometimes I caught her in those holiday moments, but couldn't
Hold her – and now regret I took the offer of a second set
Of prints and not another roll of film. Those photos are
Somewhere in this house, and – to this day – remain unframed.

8. La Belle Dame

*she wakes and/begins to weep//as he cries himself/to sleep//
to dream/of nightingales// when blackbirds/are warbling//
in the morning heat*
– Ray Liversidge

Sans merci I put her to the sword
seven times no less, equalling the effort
of that Disney mouse who slew seven giants
in *Mickey & the Beanstalk*. Of course it wasn't true –
the slaying of the giants that is –
but that didn't stop the suspension of disbelief
in the village. It was a time of innocence, a time
of fear and loss, a time for heroes. And so

I galloped into her teenage dreams –
not on a charger, but valiant nonetheless!
I was homesick for something I had
never found: a Pre-Raphaelite beauty
in Post-Modern times. And that is why
I come back into these woods:
to kiss her in four places,
to silence the nightingale,
to make sure the blackbird never sings.

NO SUSPICIOUS CIRCUMSTANCES

2012

no suspicious circumstances
portraits of poets (dead)

poems by RAY LIVERSIDGE
illustrations by KATHRYN BOWDEN

Singing in chains like the sea
(Portrait of Dylan Thomas)[3]

I begin with you, boily boy, boyhood hero,
Self-acclaimed Rimbaud of Cwmdonkin Drive,
Tomb-rooting, womb-raiding, welshing boyo
Who knew buggerall Welsh, yet grew to give
Your tongue the mother of all hidings with
Bardic, bawdy hwyl and yawp, syntactical high jinks.
Between words it was beers at Brown's with the wife
Until America inveigled the Poet Inc.
Then you did the rest with a biblical best eighteen stiff drinks.

---

[3] Generally regarded as the greatest Welsh poet, Dylan Thomas was born in Swansea in 1914. Although criticised for often making more sound than sense, he wrote many fine poems. One of his best-loved works is the play for voices *Under Milk Wood*. His last words reputedly were: 'I have just had eighteen whiskeys in a row. I do believe that is a record.' However, the story is probably apocryphal. He died from the effects of alcohol in New York on 9 November 1953.

The path ends where the wood ends
(Portrait of Edward Thomas)[4]

Like Dylan, you died in your thirty-ninth year.
Like Dylan, born with the same name, the same
Urge to live the writer's life, however austere.
Yet, to you, nature was no metaphor, feigned
Or fabled dingle; but dell, down, wind and rain
Of your beloved Hampshire. Robert Frost moved next door.
So did the war. More than a hundred poems came.
In one you *stepped out ... into an April morning*, called
Into a dark and cloistered wood on your last Wordsworthian walk.

---

[4] Edward Thomas was born in 1878 in London to Welsh parents. Although a Georgian poet he wrote with a modern sensibility about the impact that time and war have on country life. Thomas enlisted in 1914 and was sent to France in early 1917. On the first day of the Battle of Arras on 9 April 1917 he was killed by a bomb blast.

No trembler in the world's storm-troubled sphere
(Portrait of Emily Brontë)[5]

Tired of the sibling saga of Angria, you
And Anne imagine another kingdom.
For *so hopeless is the world without*, you
Withdraw to a *world within*, bereft of men
And friends, heather on the moor your kith and kin.
Your mother dies, two sisters too, and then your brother.
When Charlotte wrings some poems out of you and Anne
You turn to prose, comment on the Yorkshire weather,
The ranny air; your soul as brave as any born to suffer.

---

[5] Emily Jane Brontë was born in Thornton, Yorkshire in 1818. Educated at home, her three sisters and brother wrote stories and poems about imaginary kingdoms of Angria and Gondal. It is believed that Emily's health was affected by unsanitary living conditions, and that a cold caught during the funeral of her brother hastened her death. Refusing any medical help she died on 19 December 1848. Emily Brontë is best known as the author of *Wuthering Heights*.

The black sheep of the moor
(Portrait of Patrick Brontë)[6]

The only son, you are the one your father had
Hope for. In your room over the Yorkshire moor
He reads you Latin texts, while in your head
Forlorn lords story from toy soldiers on the floor.
At Thorp Green you cannot hold a job: and the more
You try to teach, the fewer lessons learned. You took
To sounding like a melancholic, drugged and drunken bore.
Having read your poems I see why Wordsworth overlooks
Them, and your sisters doodled your name in the margins
of their notebooks.

---

[6] Patrick Branwell Brontë was born in Thornton, Yorkshire in 1817. The only brother of Charlotte, Emily and Anne, he was regarded, in his childhood and youth, as the most talented of the children. Although he was a heavy drinker at the time, it was thought that a failed love affair in his twenties caused him to sink into further drunkenness, drugs, debt and despair. He died from tuberculosis on 24 September 1848.

All that jazz
(Portrait of Hart Crane)[7]

O bright-eyed, beautiful, all-American boy!
Life was one big speak-easy of booze and casual sax,
Boys like candy for the taking from your father's store.
Striated with nuances, nervosities, your text
Struts and frets, spawns a bridge, constructs a matrix
Of steel and glass, a *delirium of jewels.*
Winter grips the bridge. Nothing works: not the Aztec
Trip, the Caribbean romp, the begging of the muse:
Your final *vernal strophe,* a *birdless silence* astern an ocean cruise.

---

[7] Hart Crane's poetry can seem obscure, as his baroque language emphasised its visionary aspect rather than seeking clarity. He is probably best known for his poem about the Brooklyn Bridge, called simply 'The Bridge', which he described as a 'mystical synthesis of America'. He was born in Ohio in 1899 and committed suicide by jumping off the deck of the SS *Orizaba* near the coast of Florida on 26 April 1932.

Days of wine and roses
(Portrait of Ernest Dowson)[8]

Posthumously, your words entered the lexicon:
Gone with the wind, the days of wine and roses,
I have been faithful to thee in my fashion.
A fashion fostered at the Rhymers' Club with losers
(Mostly), and ignorant writers looking down their noses
At the pubescent daughter of a Polack. *Desolate
And sick of an old passion*, you cut your losses
As absinthe fails to make the *tart grow fonder*. Yet
You buy a drink; toast again arrested development, arrested sex.

---

[8] Ernest Dowson was born in London in 1867. He was a member of the Rhymers' Club which included W. B. Yeats, and his work is associated with the Decadent movement. When Dowson was in his early 20s he fell in love with the 11-year-old daughter of a Polish restaurant owner. He courted Adelaide ('Missie') for many years, but his love remained unrequited. When she married a tailor who lodged above her father's restaurant, Dowson was heartbroken. For the last two years of his life, he lived in sordid supper-houses and died of alcoholism on 23 February 1900.

A name writ in water
(Portrait of John Keats)[9]

Barely taller than a stable door, you saw
Into the dark but chose deliberate happiness.
To some, you crassly slobbered on a sweet-shop window;
Yet, when all the sweets are gone... O such fine excess!
Such beauty, such aching pleasure in the transience.
As leaves to a tree your poems came naturally; and if
We hear your voice in Nature's music, we catch the weariness,
The fever, and the fret in your luxuriant breath.
Forever panting, forever young, forever half in love with love...
and death.

---

[9] John Keats was born in London in 1795. His father worked as a hostler at the stables attached to the Swan and Hoop Inn. Although his poems were not generally well received by critics in his lifetime, Keats is now one of the most popular English poets. He had a somewhat fraught relationship with Frances (Fanny) Brawne. Because of his poor health, lack of finances and dim prospects, their love remained unconsummated. Keats died of tuberculosis in Rome on 23 February 1821.

Rilke's wingman
(Portrait of Sidney Keyes)[10]

From birth, death commanded your attention;
From a field forever England to a 'friend' from Germany.
Handed to a grandfather, suckled by a nurse,
You spent your youth in quiet husbandry:
Animals, birds, trees… books of poetry.
Then Rilke's angel swept, spread its bony wings,
And knocked the lot into the bin of history.
From the front you wrote of a time when the time for speaking
Returns, then passed through a gate into a wilderness, to die, to sing.

---

[10] Sydney Keyes was born in Kent, England, in 1922, His early poetry was influenced by nature and the Romantics. After he visited France in 1939 his poetry became more symbolic with, for example, birds and animals bearing the significance of deeper values. He entered the army in April 1942 and was killed by the Germans in Tunisia a year later on 29 April after only two weeks of active service.

Piss elegant flâneur
(Portrait of Shelton Lea)[11]

You never got to the chocolates because
You never saw the boiled lollies! You copped the blame
Just the same and a good walloping in due course.
The only decent thing they gave you was your name.
Always our Shelley – but never ours – you came
And went as you pleased, seeking beauty outside the law.
Roll another number, serenade again the *grande dame*
In that peach melba hat, *piss elegant flâneur*,
Then *choof on through to the bar*, dark minstrel, bright troubadour.

---

[11] Shelton Lea was born Philip Anthony Roberts in 1946 at the Haven, a home for un-married mothers in North Fitzroy. As an infant he was adopted by Monty and Valerie Lea, part of the Darrell Lea confectionery dynasty. Valerie showed no love or affection for her adopted son. Shelton ran away from home and spent periods of time in boys' homes and jails. Poetry was his life, and he was a legendary performer in Melbourne, Australia. He died from the effects of hard living on 13 May 2005.

God's parle with dust
(Portrait of Charlotte Mew)[12]

Amidst the poverty, insanity and death,
A sisterly pact of celibacy to stem
Dysgenic blood. Body waiving what the soul inherits.
And though His arms are full of broken things, to Him
She turns in times of doubt, yet doubts the wisdom
Of her turning. To perfume the fetid air
Of the nursing home, a rose, a geranium,
Disinfectant. To God she gifts a lock of hair,
Then attends the tendrils of her dark and unruly hair.

---

[12] Charlotte Mew was born in London in 1869. Her father died when she was young, leaving the family in financial difficulties. As her family had a history of mental illness Charlotte and her sister, Anne, decided never to marry for fear of passing on insanity to their children. Her poetry explores spiritual values through sensual imagery, and her use of language was unusual and experimental for its time. When Anne died, Charlotte sank into depression and was admitted to a nursing home, where she took her own life by drinking Lysol on 24 March 1928.

Puttin' on the Ritz
(Portrait of Edna St Vincent Millay)[13]

Her head is turned from the camera, and she looks
Somewhat winsome among the magnolia blossom:
Like a mischievous minx who's just swallowed two figs;
A girl who becomes – and flaunts – it; a woman
Who *will touch a hundred flowers and not pick one.*
Oh, she is loved; but there are new kids on the block.
(Even Edmund Wilson misses her *old imperial line.*)
She shoots up, she drinks, she sways, she falls and breaks her neck –
The ghostly rain and *quiet pain* slowly drowning all memory and sex.

---

[13] Born in Maine in 1892, Edna St Vincent Millay was one of America's most read and beloved poets in the 1920s and was hailed as the female voice of her generation. In 1923 she became the first woman to win the Pulitzer Prize. In the poem "First Fig" she wrote: 'My candle burns at both ends'. And that was the way she lived. She died on 19 October 1950 after falling – or throwing herself – down the stairs at her home.

The art of dying
(Portrait of Sylvia Plath)[14]

You are the one who cried out to be done:
A given, given the criteria
That I set. And yet, reading your poems again
I sense calm amidst the hysteria.
Those final lines written in suburbia,
In the brumal mornings before the housewife
Played her role with the suicide inside her.
Evening was falling on the unattended beehives
When they demanded you go in a blaze of glory, a sunset of knives.

There was no blaze of glory, sunset of knives –
Simply an eclipse in a cloud of gas
In the cauldron of morning before the kids would rise.
And how fresh and far now his first rough kiss,
Your teeth on his cheek, the swelling ring-moat of tooth-marks,
The blood drawn drawing you into his dark galaxy,
The cold interstellar spaces of your universes.
Let scholars squabble over missing diaries;
Just give me poetry, give me blood: the blood jet that is poetry.

---

[14] Sylvia Plath was born in Jamaica Plain, Massachusetts, in 1932. In 1956 she won a Fulbright scholarship to Cambridge, where she met the English poet Ted Hughes. Their relationship has been the subject of much discussion, especially in regard to her suicide on 11 February 1963. Along with Anne Sexton, Plath is associated with the genre of confessional poetry initiated by Robert Lowell and W. D. Snodgrass.

Once upon a midnight dreary
(Portrait of Edgar Allan Poe)[15]

'Tel qu'en lui-même enfin l'éternité le change'.
Two days before, befuddled, sluing the streets
Of Baltimore, dressed in the clothes of a stranger.
Such an ending he could write in his sleep.
So, what had Baudelaire and Mallarmé seen
America did not? Beyond a chamber door,
The *discordant melody* of an ominous raven,
The moment of birth, the unforgiving storm,
The beautiful, cruel cold fists of ice seizing the Boston harbour.

---

[15] Better known for his short stories of the macabre than for his poetry, Edgar Allan Poe did, however, write the well-known poem "The Raven". After his death his reputation suffered, mainly due to the rumour-mongering of one man, Rufus Griswold. Poe was born in Boston, Massachusetts, in 1809 and died in mysterious circumstances on 7 October 1849.

Poète maudit
(Portrait of Arthur Rimbaud)[16]

So, brass ensorcells trumpet, wood a violin!
And he, enfant terrible, sure is something else.
Not for him the pubescent pursuit of torturing
Insects behind his mother's back, back fences.
The punk loused up, got toxic, fucked his senses,
Tore down the veil from every mystery.
In Paris, Verlaine shoots and asks no questions,
Chucks the kid's poems drunkenly up the creek, turning banal
His world; a world so hideously beautiful, so scourged, anal.

---

[16] Arthur Rimbaud was born in the provincial town of Charleville, France, in 1854. A precocious child, he had virtually written his manifesto on poetry by the age of 16. Three years later he totally abandoned his arcane art after a debauched 18 months in Paris which culminated in his lover, Verlaine, shooting him in the arm. He died on 10 November 1891 following complications after having his leg amputated.

Gravity and waggery
(Portrait of Christopher Smart)[17]

In the Age of Reason you just had to be mad:
Cross-dressing as Mary Midnight, hitting the bars,
Praying in public places, being a lad,
Punching out poems of unconditional praise.
'I'd as lief pray with Kit Smart as anyone else',
Dr Johnson declared – but he was not your quack!
When Anna runs off with the kids you return to grace
Your prison walls with poems. Crazy, or not,
We give thanks for your song, and the adventures of Jeoffrey the cat.

---

[17] Christopher Smart, born in 1722 in Kent, England, spent several years in asylums mainly because his habit of praying out loud in public was considered irrational behaviour. His "A Song to David" is considered one of the most original and powerful religious poems of the eighteenth century. Smart died penniless in a debtors' prison on 21 May 1771.

We are all in the gutter, but some of us are looking at the stars
(Portrait of Oscar Wilde)[18]

Before and after the essays and plays, poesy
Bookended a dogma of cultivated leisure,
The useless luxury of a life with Bosie,
The sleeping with panthers, the panic the pleasure.
Letting your guard down, old Queensberry measures
His blow… and you stagger as an ox to the shambles.
No sun shines, yet light breaks as you suffer
In a sorry cell. Then, in a seedy room you gamble
On the wallpaper outlasting you. The pattern, like love, unspeakable.

---

[18] Oscar Fingal O'Flahertie Wills Wilde was born in Dublin in 1854. He wrote in many genres, but is best remembered as a playwright and a master of one-liners. Wilde sued the Marquess of Queensberry (the father of his lover Lord Alfred "Bosie" Douglas) for libel after Queensberry accused him of sodomy. Wilde was convicted of gross indecency and imprisoned for two years. In prison he wrote De Profundis, an 80-page letter about suffering and spiritual struggles which is a dark counterpoint to his earlier philosophy of pleasure. After his release he left for France, where he wrote his last work, the long poem "The Ballad of Reading Gaol". He died in penury in Paris on 30 November 1900.

ORADOUR-SUR-GLANE

2017

Oradour-sur-Glane

Visitors enter the ruins
From the opposite direction
To the route taken into the village
By the 2nd SS Panzer Division.
From the Centre de la Mémorie
The narrow road rises
With a low, intact retaining wall
On the left, and a number of
Rubbled walls of varying height
On the other side.

No number of history lessons
Or sum of research can ready you
For arrival at road's end
And that moment of catching
Breath in a blistered world of
Six hundred and forty-two
Moments of unbreathing.

Both names mean on a river.
So, one can understand
How a stranger might easily
Misread a road sign or
Mistake one town for the other:
Oradour-sur-Glane,
Oradour-sur-Vayres.
Life at times a lottery.

      * * *

There's a slant of light –
Of that is certain –
A slant of melting light –
The heft of hurting.

It cracks the stained-glass windows,
It splits the wooden pews,
It fills the vessels of the heart,
It destroys – and it renews.

I am the window that opens on the world.
Concentrated in this holy place
Fear sings in us like wires.
Insects sounding in our children's chests

Are concentrated in this holy place.
I am the sacred witness from the church
Of insects sounding in my child's chest.
I am a mother who has lost everything.

The sacrilegers of the church
Stuff smoking doves into the lungs of mothers –
I am another mother who's lost everything.
I came out alive from the crematory oven,

Releasing doves from the lungs of mothers.
Fear sang in us like wires
But I came out alive from the crematory oven.
I am the window opening on the world.

How easy to imagine death to be
Like travelling alone in a car on a balmy night –
With all the windows down –
And the thought of home
Where life is rumoured to reside.

Suddenly, unnumbered shades of the underworld
Already a commonwealth of flesh.

This is the woman you never can be.
We know that, but we love her anyway:
Her *savoir vivre,* her strut, her smile,
Every single thing about her
That never was. Yet, such is our love
Her tiny body grows into the shape
Of a beautiful nothingness
With chestnut hair just like her mother's.

And so we feed her, not with food
But with the thought that she might pass
Over as one unfallen in an unfallen world.

She is looking in a mirror at a woman
Who never was, a beautiful woman
In a wedding dress she never will wear.

If only a healing chorale could rebuild
The nests of bewildered swallows,
Lift the fallen fruit back to their branches,
Return the babies to their prams,
Unlight the fires, cancel the commands,
Return the bullets to the barrels of their guns.

   * * *

The photo is taken on
The 23rd of June 1940,
Nine days after the fall
Of Paris and one day after
France accepts defeat.
We know this because
It is the only time
He visited the city.

Himself, a frustrated and
Pedestrian artist, he
Positions himself
Between the architect
Albert Speer
And the sculptor
Arno Breker –
Between the Nazi who
Says sorry at the Nuremberg
Trials and the shaper of
Wucht und Willenhaftigkeit.
Hitler stares directly
Into the lens of the camera,
The Eiffel Tower behind him.
It still stands.

Florence Gould did not know
Much about literature, but she knew
How to entertain writers.
Her salons at lunchtime on Thursdays
Brought together the French
The Americans and the Germans
To talk literature and politics…
And to gossip.

Had everyone heard the latest
About Gertrude and Alice?
What about that Hemingway fellow
With his machismo all over the shop?
And that photo of Chevalier
Drinking from a bottle of Vichy water.
Maybe the Germans in the corner
Of the room are discussing
The twenty-two hundred tonnes
Of books burned, or the twenty-two
Thousand stolen *objects d' art.*
And what could Cocteau and Colette

Possibly be saying to that Gestapo officer
Between sips of cognac?
In Paris, not everyone was encumbered
By the German occupation.
Some welcomed the strangers
To their unoccupied zones.
For a collaboration horizontale.
'My heart is French,'
The actress is rumoured
To have quipped.
'But my ass is international.'

In the face of peril
And under threat, poetry
Cries out, accuses, waits.
In Paul Éluard's poem
Liberty's name is written
Again and again and again
On all manner of thing;
A single copy sent to London
For printing, and 'Liberté'
Is let fly like paper pigeons
By the RAF
In the tens of thousands
All over France.

Like acts of love
Spot fires break out
But Paris refuses to burn,
Quashing Hitler's *schadenfreude*.
Meanwhile, on the 25th of August
General Charles De Gaulle –
Better at mobilizing myths than troops –
Addresses the crowd from the Hôtel de Ville,
Declaring Paris liberated, and
France the only, the real, *l'éternel*.

Visitors exit the ruins
From the opposite direction
To the route taken into the village
By the 2nd SS Panzer Division,
Down the narrow road which rises
With a low, intact retaining wall
On the right, and a number of
Rubbled walls of varying height
On the other side to the
Centre de la Mémorie.

No number of history lessons
Or sum of research could have
Prepared you for what you
Have just witnessed,
And that moment of catching
Breath in a blistered world of
Six hundred and forty-two
Moments of unbreathing.

...OF A SUDDEN

2023

One wonders

why they reside here
when the deck chairs on
the balconies remain empty
while the river below the
hills storied with houses
is begging to be beheld.

The river – rightly indifferent –
does what rivers do: slips
out unnoticed to the ocean,
birdsong at its back.

Sometimes I don't feel comfortable writing

about something which might end tragically, like the time I complacently likened the shrill laughter of teenagers inside the cabin of the speeding vehicle to hubcaps bouncing down a highway before losing control of the narrative and having the head of the driver shatter the windscreen.

It is hoped this story

will appeal to those interested in the four humours of Hippocratic medicine, which was the commonly held view of the human body among European physicians until the advent of modern medical research in the 19th century.

In the first decade of the 20th century, the Irish writer James Joyce – either frustrated with its conventional structure or furious at publishers who ignored it – tossed the manuscript of *Stephen Hero* into a fire. Apparently, his wife, Nora, and his sister, Eileen, saved part of the document which would later be retitled *A Portrait of the Artist as a Young Man*.

In the same decade of the 21st century, a frustrated and furious Australian writer threw the pages of his poetry manuscript into the Southern Ocean.

At the same time, a Latin American writer – either frustrated or furious – was surreptitiously slipping the notebooks containing his short stories into his own coffin, which would soon be lowered into a grave in Cartagena de Indias.

Meanwhile, an English writer – neither frustrated nor furious – was systematically saving the versions of everything he wrote to the cloud.

Imagine if you can this story

beginning at 8:16 AM on a Friday when the middle-aged vice-president of an insurance company (immaculately attired in a three-piece pinstripe suit) is walking to his office in a city in Connecticut. Try to picture a casually dressed non-mercantile man walking along the same street in the opposite direction the next morning to, perhaps, purchase a newspaper. See how both men drop a piece of paper they have, at that moment, taken out of their trouser pockets. How both bend over to retrieve the paper scraps from the sidewalk, then look at what is in their hands.

One note reads: money is a kind of poetry. The other: poetry is the supreme fiction.

She had positioned herself

in society so as to be able to write full time, and had published several books, including a new and selected. Her poems were usually about love and loss and longing, and she had nurtured a reputation as a major minor poet. She was quite content with her achievement to date, but now she had writer's block. She had not written a poem in over a year.

As she lived in a leafy outer suburb, a literary friend suggested she try her hand at ecopoetry. The poems came – as Keats said they should – as naturally as leaves to a tree. Within a matter of months, she had enough for a manuscript. After ringing her agent to discuss her new book, she went outside and commenced cultivating her garden, using the pages of her manuscript as compost.

Ask you (said quickly)

I can't get it to go
Upright. It lies on its side
And no amount of coaxing
Will make it erect.
Sometimes things aren't black
And white. Sometimes they're grey
And despite the fingering
It refuses to rise.
It's like a game of cat
And mouse, and the mouse
Loses, and the cat (hopefully
Out of the bag by now) is content
To lie there with me with a bucket
Of popcorn and view
The moving world obliquely.

She said:

For someone who writes poetry you sure don't say much.

He said: The silence between words carries as much weight as the words themselves.

The next day she cleared out her wardrobe and left a scrap of paper on the kitchen table on which she had written a two-word poem.

He loved live theatre and bled easily.

She had never had a blood nose and preferred the cinema.

He was gifted with a hand that wrote in a cursive script.

Most of her messages were by text.

There was a significant age difference, and they frequently argued.

On one occasion, after a heated exchange, he commenced writing a letter seeking her forgiveness for his behaviour the previous evening. By mid-morning the temperature was already 30 degrees Celsius. Before he could lift a finger to depress the left nostril a trickle of blood dropped onto the third page of his letter. He looked down at the blurred script, the broken narrative. With his thumb he smeared blood on all the pages to give his story more gravitas.

After reading the first sentence of his letter, she decided to end the relationship and left the house to see a film. *Nosferatu* was showing at her local cinema. A week later she started dating a vampire.

'What side of the bed do you want?' he asked her.

'What do you mean?' she replied.

'Left, or right?'

'Depends on which way you're looking at the bed.'

'Head to foot.'

'We haven't even done anything yet.'

'I'm thinking of afterwards.'

'Does it matter?'

'I just have a preference, that's all,' he said, removing his shoes.

'Is it that important?'

'I have a medical condition.'

'A medical condition?'

'I need to lie on my right side on the right-hand side of the bed.'

'That means then that you'll be right next to the bedroom door,' she said, reclasping her bra. 'So, when you put your shoes back on, you go out that door and turn right, and you'll find the front door. And if it's all right with you, would you please lock the door when you've left.'

White angels

In twilight moments
He numbers them,

Like counting sheep.
But he's not enticing sleep

(Although he nods off anywhere:
A couch; a car; a chair).

And today as we take tea
He says he's counted seventy-five.

Seventy-five different
White cabbage butterflies,

Or the same butterfly
Seventy-five times?

No matter, to him, they're
His very own white angels

Which hover over his roses
In the early summer sun.

I have put the child

to sleep, she said, getting into bed.

Just like James Joyce boasted what he did with language, he said, turning off the light.

The parents woke early the next morning to discover a note pinned to the head of the cot and the child missing.

Requiem

Our daily walk takes longer now.
But you still insist on
Passing through the cemetery
With its ever-growing
Number of headstones.
You taught her grandmother
When we lived in Warrnambool
You tell me again. And his son,
You repeat, never returned from
The war in Vietnam.
And, as is our habit, we stop
To rest at the rotunda
Where, as usual, you turn
Away from the babies' graves.
And I respectfully deflect
The trembling requiem.

Since 2011 Melbourne, Australia, has

often been named the world's most liveable city. Its central business district is renowned for its laneways and its alfresco dining. It also has several lanes, such as AC/DC and Hosier, which feature street art. Here, you won't find work known as tagging, but art by acclaimed street artists such as Banksy. A number of Banksy stencils have been damaged or destroyed by deliberate and inadvertent acts. Some argue that these artefacts are great cultural losses, others that street art is not owned by anyone and is, by nature, ephemeral. However, a discussion such as this belongs in another story.

In this story, I want to tell you of the time I visited Melbourne in 2016 and, while on a tour of its laneways, came across a one-line story by American writer Alex Epstein scribbled on a wall. The story is called 'Fiction' and it goes: 'And the last man in the world is writing a novel.' Underneath the story, written in a different hand, is: 'So, obviously, he will have to self-publish.' And underneath that, in yet another script, is the quote: 'What's the intended print run?'

The last story in *Lunar Savings Time* – the same book in which "Fiction" appears – is called "Compendium of Most Snowflakes", and it too is comprised of one line which reads: 'The last man in the world wrote the last haiku in the world.' I thought that was especially clever as everybody knows poetry doesn't sell.

For him every month is

you know like cruel like it is now in april with the sun beating down on his face in jack kerouac alley & later when theres like you know no sun theres city lights & its like wow look at the lights man & then its like another alley another lane another whatever (but that's like what he likes coz its not cool @ home you know) & then from the second level of vesuvio i see his t-shirt I EAT PUSSY LIKE A KID EATS CAKE & i think thats like not cool man & how mallarmé you know wanted like removed from the lexicon & as i point my iphone @ you a voice behind me says hey you know that aint cool dude & hes you know more than like right you know

She lived in the moment and had no sense of history.

She also once had an eye for property and a liking for spices. She owned houses and apartments in many countries – including her birthplace, Holland – but lost them all when the global financial crisis hit. She now lived in a tenement in Manhattan. She once owned the tenement but had offloaded it to an Englishman for a small Indonesian island to mitigate her debt. It was a condition of the property exchange that the Dutchwoman live with the Englishman.

She was in the kitchen adding nutmeg and other spices to the evening meal. When she heard the door open, she knew what was coming. 'Hi hon, I'm home.' First, the sound of the fridge door opening and closing, the top coming off a bottle of beer, then footsteps on the tiled floor. Standing over the cooktop, she felt her body brace itself for when he would place his hand on her hip, lean over her shoulder, sniff and whisper: 'Trying to spice up our lives, eh?'

Then, over time, she lost the taste for spices. She would spend the rest of her life on Pulau Run.

~~CORONAVIRUSDISEASE – 20~~19

On my walk it stalks me.
Playful as a pup, it flits
and skips in the clippings
from yesterday's mowing of
the reserve behind my house.
Dancing in front or back,
it maintains its social distancing,
the wagtail's tail wagging like
a scripting quill. The sound of its call
like muted keys of a typewriter,
touch typing on a keyboard.

I miss the feel of you
and the sound of your voice.

He hinted he might consider moving

if she promised an ocean, or, at least, a river view. After not hearing from her, he returned to the story and noted the unhandy cadence of its first sentence. He made a promise to himself to rewrite the opening.

When she read the draft of his story, she sent him a river in an envelope. A week later he received a parcel. When he opened it, an ocean flooded his lounge room. After that he never heard from her again, and he never did get around to rewriting the beginning, or, for that matter, finishing the

www.ingramcontent.com/pod-product-compliance
Lightning Source LLC
Chambersburg PA
CBHW062214080426
42734CB00010B/1881